AWAKENING SPRING'S CREATIVITY

A Guide to Creative Freedom for Neurodivergent, Chronically Ill, and Disabled Storytellers

JESSICA WHITE

Copyright © 2025 Jessica White
All rights reserved.
ISBN: 979-8-9850266-3-4

No part of this book may be reproduced in any form or by any electronic or mechanical means, including information storage and retrieval systems, without permission in writing from the author. The only exception is by a reviewer, who may quote brief excerpts in a review.

DEDICATION

For the storytellers like me, who wrestle more with themselves than the page. May you know you are the powerful healers the world needs.

Table of Contents

Invitation to Rewrite the Rules of Creativity............x

CHAPTER 1: Breaking Free-A Spring Experiment..1

   THE MYTH: Spring Instantly Comes Alive 1

   THE TRUTH: Our Minds & Bodies Awaken Slowly..4

   OUR LIBERATION: Reclaiming Our Natural Rhythms...7

CHAPTER 2: Finding the Cyclical Path...................14

   THE MYTH: Energy Should Flow Steadily...........14

   THE TRUTH: Creativity Ebbs & Flows...................17

   OUR LIBERATION: Moving Through Spring with Agency 22

CHAPTER 3: Creating on Our Own Terms...............33

   THE MYTH: A Creative Schedule is Essential 33

   THE TRUTH: Our Capacity Changes Every Day.38

   OUR LIBERATION: Designing Our Creative Space 42

CHAPTER 4: Embodying Our Stories 50

   THE MYTH: Creativity is a Mental Activity 50

THE TRUTH: Our Bodies Birth Our Stories 54

OUR LIBERATION: Body-Friendly Creative Practices 58

CHAPTER 5: Freeing Up Energy and Attention 66

THE MYTH: Our Attention Should be Focused .. 66

THE TRUTH: We're Pattern & Relationship Creators 69

OUR LIBERATION: Redefining What We Can Create 72

CHAPTER 6: Being Kind to Our Creative Selves ... 80

THE MYTH: Our Worth Depends on What We Create 80

THE TRUTH: Self-Validation Leads to Better Story 86

OUR LIBERATION: Compassionate Creative Journaling 93

CHAPTER 7: Creating Story in Community 106

THE MYTH: Real Artists Work Alone 106

THE TRUTH: Creativity Thrives in Connection 111

OUR LIBERATION: Building Supportive Creative Networks 114

CHAPTER 8: Growing Stories in Spring 124

THE MYTH: Go Big or Go Home 124

THE TRUTH: Matching Our Projects to Our Resources 129

OUR LIBERATION: Finding Freedom In Project Alignment 135

CHAPTER 9: When Creating Feels Impossible 146

THE MYTH: Creative Blocks Mean We are Lazy 146

THE TRUTH: Creative Barriers Are Complex .. 150

OUR LIBERATION: Staying Creative Beyond Output 154

CHAPTER 10: Healing Our Stories 162

THE MYTH: Creation Is About Publication, Recognition, & Profit 162

THE TRUTH: Stories Heal & Liberate 167

OUR LIBERATION: Storytelling for Liberation 171

CHAPTER 11: Preparing for Summer's Intensity 178

THE MYTH: We Should Enter Summer Full Throttle 178

THE TRUTH: Thoughtful Transitions Protect Creativity 181

OUR LIBERATION: Setting Boundaries for Creative Well-being 184

FAREWELL: Our Ongoing Journey 191

Invitation to Rewrite the Rules of Creativity

"The creation of a thousand forests is in one acorn."
— Ralph Waldo Emerson

Conventional advice paints an idealistic picture of storytellers waking at dawn, sitting in front of their computer, and pushing through their physical and mental discomfort until they produce work.

But these rules were designed for linear minds and able bodies. Ones that thrive on external pressure to reach their peak performance. For those who are neurodivergent, chronically ill, or disabled, this advice doesn't just fail us, it shackles us with shame. Experts convince us that if our energy ebbs and flows, if we require rest, or novelty, or special accommodations, then we're broken and we'll never become serious storytellers.

That is a lie. And it's time for us to break free.

Nature offers a different model — one of liberation, not restriction. Spring doesn't force itself into being. It does not bloom on command. It awakens when the conditions are right, responding to warmth, light, and nourishment. Some seeds sprout early, while others wait, lingering under the soil until their moment comes. None of them are wrong. None of them are failures.

And neither are we for not blooming under conditions that do not fit our needs.

This season is not about forcing creativity into rigid molds, but about emergence. It's about shaking off the myths that have kept us trapped. It's about experimenting with new ways of creating that honor our natural rhythms and core values. It's about allowing our stories to rise, stretch toward the light, and take their unique forms.

We are not creators who need to replicate the masters or follow a road paved by others. We are storytellers who are led by their inner light off the beaten path. It's time to create in ways that honor our divergent minds, our disabled bodies, and our lived experiences. This book is not just a guide — it is an act of joyful reclamation of our creative lives.

I invite you to join me in this season of liberation to rewrite the rules by which we create stories. To free yourself up to grow, pause, and flourish creatively on your own terms.

When you're ready, turn the page.

CHAPTER 1: Breaking Free- A Spring Experiment

"In the embrace of spring, the world becomes a garden of endless possibilities." — Unknown

THE MYTH: Spring Instantly Comes Alive

Every year, around Valentine's Day, stores fill their shelves with spring-themed items. Advertisements flood our feeds, encouraging us to start fresh, chase goals, and become better versions of ourselves. But this push for renewal has little to do with the actual transition of seasons.

In nature, spring emerges gradually. The days grow longer, temperatures fluctuate, plants sprout, and animals slowly leave their dens. It's rarely a sudden shift. Even we hesitate to pack away winter clothes or adjust our thermostats, unsure if spring has truly arrived. Yet, societal advice urges us to commit and act quickly, afraid we'll miss our chance to grow or succeed.

THE EXPECTATION TO FEEL ENERGIZED & PRODUCTIVE

Spring is frequently framed as one of renewed vitality. Messages like "Now's the time to bloom!" or "Emerge from your cocoon!" sound harmless. But they reinforce the belief that ties our worth to how much we produce.

As storytellers whose minds and bodies operate beyond the neurotypical and non-disabled paradigms, we face a choice. We can contort ourselves to fit these external expectations. Or we can claim our *sovereign* right to create according to our natural rhythms.

Sovereignty is the right to govern yourself and your actions. Unfortunately, modern culture pressures us to follow the crowd. Even in creative spaces, there's a constant challenge to write faster, produce more, and stay relevant.

But do we have to follow these rules? And, more importantly, do they serve us?

WHEN ADVICE IGNORES OUR ENERGETIC SHIFTS

Often we feel simultaneously drawn to the slow unfolding energy of spring while also feeling crushed by the demand for productivity. I call this phenomenon *Seasonal Dissonance*. This clash between what our bodies need and what others expect can overwhelm us.

This dissonance shows up as:

- Shame when others seem energized while we feel depleted.
- Frustration when our body can't match our creative ambitions.
- Worry when our project timeline is "behind" schedule.
- Grief when physical limitations impact our creative routines.

When we push ourselves to create on-demand, burnout usually follows. If the advice we're following leads to seasonal dissonance, it's a sign something isn't aligned with how our minds and bodies work. Those feelings of shame, frustration, and exhaustion aren't personal failures. They're signals calling us to pause and reassess.

THE DANGER OF FORCED PRODUCTIVITY

The expectation to continually produce stories affects all creatives. The pressure and shame of failing can lead to imposter syndrome or harsh inner criticism when we compare ourselves to our peers.

For neurodivergent and disabled storytellers, it hits harder. Unlike the steady energy levels many people assume are the norm, our energy is often unpredictable. Forcing productivity can lead to mental and physical pushback, leaving us depleted.

Attempting to create the perfect environment or ideal circumstances often drains us before we even begin. Instead of writing, we use up our time, energy, attention, and space to meet external expectations.

These pressures can also worsen existing challenges. Too many choices may cause decision fatigue or analysis paralysis, leaving us stuck. Advice, like joining an in-person writing group, might require resources we simply don't have.

But if we forgo the route that works for neurotypical and able-bodied storytellers, what path should we travel?

THE TRUTH: Our Minds & Bodies Awaken Slowly

The beauty of our divergent brains and disabled bodies isn't their proximity to what's considered "normal." It's their alignment with the rhythms of nature that modern society has disconnected us from.

HOW SPRING AFFECTS US

Our "symptoms" are actually *Truth Signals* — insights from our bodies that guide us toward what we need.

Many of us experience heightened sensitivity, which may show up as:

- Predicting weather changes hours before meteorologists.
- Detecting subtle shifts in energy in other people or environments.
- Feeling stronger effects on our capacity when the hours of sunlight increase or decrease.

When we listen to these signals, we can choose actions aligned with our resources and abilities that better serve us.

PERSONAL SEASONAL SHIFTS

As someone with ADHD, I see all the potential of spring. However, all the possibilities scatter my focus, making it hard to prioritize and take action. During this season, my energy is best used for curating inspiration and exploring new ideas that will carry me into the more active summer months.

I also live with chronic migraines. The unpredictable weather keeps me bedridden for half of the month. While medication reduces the pain, it doesn't restore my brain's capacity to function. Pushing myself because I can tolerate the discomfort actually delays my recovery.

Rigid schedules once left me overwhelmed and stuck. Decision fatigue and executive dysfunction pulled me further from my creative goals. Instead of writing, I either escaped into world-building or avoided my projects altogether.

But now I lean into my energy shifts, following them instead of arbitrary calendars. I respect the signals of stress and overwhelm my body sends.

WHY THIS SEASON IS DIFFICULT FOR MANY OF US

While no two neurodivergent brains or disabled bodies are the same, many of us experience seasonal challenges. Spring brings a surge of energy, but also sensory overload and heightened physical responses. Some even experience Seasonal Affective Disorder (SAD) not only in winter but in spring due to sudden environmental changes.

We must remember, our perceptions and experiences aren't flaws to eliminate or problems to solve. They're signals pointing us toward what we need. By recognizing our natural rhythms, we can reclaim spring as a season of experimentation. We can listen to our bodies instead of pushing them to conform to external expectations.

In truth, we are not separate from nature, we're part of it. Like the plants and animals around us, we flourish when we align with the changing world around us. This interconnection stands in contrast to the productivity-obsessed mindset that encourages constant output.

But how do we honor this connection within our creative lives?

Journal Reflection: *When did you first realize that standard creative advice wasn't compatible with a mind or body like yours? What wisdom has your body offered that other people dismissed? How might you begin to listen to those signals without judgment?*

OUR LIBERATION: Reclaiming Our Natural Rhythms

Spring's arrival isn't a sudden burst of productivity. It's a slow and steady awakening. In nature, bulbs push through frozen soil, trees cautiously bud, and animals emerge, testing their surroundings. This deliberate pace is nature's wisdom at work — and it can be ours too.

The cultural narrative tells us this season is for hustling, but true growth comes from experimentation, not pressure. Some seeds thrive, while others never sprout. This is not failure. It's how ecosystems flourish. Likewise, our imagination blooms best when we allow curiosity and rest to coexist.

As storytellers with rebellious brains and bodies, spring invites us away from quickly creating lots of viable content. Instead, it challenges us to embody a radical shift from production to experimentation.

Instead of focusing solely on productivity, this season invites us to try new things without attachment to the outcome. Explore unfamiliar genres, play with unconventional storytelling techniques, or write simply for the joy of it. We don't have to compromise our values or energetic well-being. We can follow what sparks our interest. Not every idea will bloom or bear fruit, and that's okay.

Just as robins gather one twig at a time to build their nests, our creative work grows through small, intentional efforts. Trust that each choice shapes something meaningful, even if the final form remains uncertain.

But how do we integrate this gentle, sovereign approach into our creative lives? How do we shift our actions from external to internal alignment? We must claim our rightful place in spring's unfolding story — one where our rhythms lead the way.

RECLAIMING OUR POWER

Despite its challenges, spring offers distinctive opportunities for neurodivergent and disabled storytellers like us. These show up in ways that align surprisingly well with our natural tendencies. However, many have been erased, or at least pushed aside, in traditional creative advice.

In spring, storytellers frequently experience what I refer to as *Inspiration Inundations*. These overwhelming floods of ideas are frequently misinterpreted as "distractions." However, for us, they're fertilizer for the soil of our creative gardens. These dreams, observations, and newfound connections are all part of this vibrant energy drawn from our sensory awareness.

Society often calls this hypersensitivity. But for neurodivergent and disabled people, it can also be hyperawareness. **We notice** shifts in light, temperature, mood, or tone. While society encourages us to numb or dismiss these experiences, they are valuable. The same hum of electrical machines that irritates us often disrupts animals and plants. The flickering lights that trigger migraines may interfere with the natural rhythms. Our heightened perception is a form of wisdom.

Chronically ill and disabled storytellers frequently experience highly developed senses of *interoception* — the ability to feel our bodies' internal signals. Indigenous cultures sometimes refer to this phenomenon as **Body Wisdom.** They believe that because we are part of nature, we are interconnected with our environment. Unlike us, they are taught to listen to instead of ignore or pathologize these internal signals.

We can listen to our body wisdom too. Our physical responses to situations can give us wisdom about how to respond. We instinctively know when we feel tightness in our chest, something is wrong. Or that when we get butterflies, we anticipate a surprise. As storytellers, these sensitivities can help us create more vivid details and metaphors that capture life in ways others don't experience.

Hypersensitivity isn't a deficit. It's an advantage in a world that has forgotten how to connect with the environment and follow nature's rhythms.

DISMANTLING SEASONAL OPPRESSION

The demand to bloom during spring mirrors a harmful form of creative colonization. This systematic pressure disregards our body's natural rhythms, urging us to produce at an externally imposed pace.

We see this mindset in industrial agriculture, where biodiversity is sacrificed for profit. Instead of nurturing a variety of crops throughout the season, industries prioritize fast-growing, uniform plants. The belief in speed and sameness seeps into our creative lives.

How often do we feel ashamed for resting when others are being productive? Or abandon creative projects because they don't fit our arbitrary schedules? If our energy dips, we're quick to blame ourselves, labeling our natural needs as failures rather than wisdom.

But our bodies aren't malfunctioning — they're speaking. Fatigue, resistance, or a desire to pause aren't signs of inadequacy. They're signals that we need to adjust our pace, tend to our well-being, and honor our own timing.

By tuning in, we reclaim our sovereignty. Our creativity isn't measured by how quickly we bloom. It's reflected in how deeply we root and grow.

Pocket Note: *Our storytelling doesn't emerge despite our neurodivergence or disability. It exists because of the liberating perspective these experiences provide.*

PRACTICE: PERMISSION SLIP FOR REST

Spring's association with output generates an internal pressure that undermines genuine creative well-being. Formal permission to rest represents not only self-care but resistance. Copy the declaration below into your favorite journal or print it out and hang it somewhere you see often.

My Spring Well-being Declaration
I, (your name), hereby claim my absolute right to:

- *Rest when productivity culture demands output.*
- *Create according to my sovereign rhythm, regardless of expectations.*
- *Establish and defend sensory boundaries without guilt or justification.*
- *Honor my body's needs and wisdom as legitimate and worthy.*
- *Define creative value through my own sovereign standards.*
- *Prioritize internal truth equally with external production.*

This sovereignty is my birthright and requires no validation.

Signed: (your name) Date:

    This declaration isn't symbolic. It's a tangible act of resistance against systems designed to override our creative well-being. It's a powerful tool for psychological safety. Display it prominently in your creative space as a reminder of your right to create on your own terms.

REFLECT: INTEGRATING SOVEREIGNTY

As we conclude this chapter, integrate its liberating framework through these reflection practices:

- Identify one aspect of spring's energy that naturally aligns with your neurodivergent or disabled experience. How might you amplify this natural alignment as a form of creative resistance?
- Name a spring productivity myth you've internalized that colonizes your authentic creative rhythm. Draft a personal counter-narrative that honors your body's actual wisdom.
- Design a simple sovereignty system to capture spring's inspiration without surrendering your energetic autonomy.
- Describe your ideal sensory conditions for liberating creation. What immediate steps can you take to establish these conditions as non-negotiable requirements?

CHAPTER 2: Finding the Cyclical Path

"The spiral in a snail's shell is the same mathematically as the spiral in the Milky Way galaxy, and it's also the same mathematically as the spirals in our DNA. It's the same ratio that you'll find in very basic music that transcends cultures all over the world." — Joseph Gordon-Levitt

THE MYTH: Energy Should Flow Steadily

CREATIVE ENERGY INCREASES CONSISTENTLY

Spring is often sold as a season of nonstop growth — a time to plant ideas, maximize productivity, and harvest results. Creative advice tends to mirror this belief, pushing us to:

- Grow our craft in a measurable way.
- Plant only our most viable ideas.
- Maintain predictable, steady output.
- Weed out distractions.
- Produce stories that can be edited and sold.

But this mindset strips away the natural rhythms that sustain creativity. Growth isn't uniform. Nature doesn't demand constant progress. Trees bud cautiously, plants bloom in their own time, and some seeds never sprout at all. Yet, conventional wisdom tells us that if we're not moving forward, we're falling behind.

THE HARM OF DISREGARDING OUR RESOURCES

For neurodivergent, chronically ill, and disabled storytellers, this model is especially harmful. It devalues the ebbs and flows of our energy. When we try to force creativity, we risk burnout, exhaustion, and disconnection from our natural rhythms. Instead of honoring our minds and bodies, we're left chasing an impossible ideal of consistent output.

This myth erases the beautiful complexity of our divergent processes and burns out our creative spirit. Its pressure is a form of creative violence. Not the dramatic kind we imagine, but the quieter, persistent force that erodes our *agency* — how, when, and why we create. When the world measures our worth by our productivity, it robs us of that freedom. We're left believing that pauses are failures and that our value is tied to how much we produce.

NATURE PROVIDES A BETTER MODEL

Nature grows in cycles that expand and contract, not straight predictable lines. Plants constantly surprise us with how they react to environmental changes. They share resources, adapt to their surroundings, and grow in response to what's needed. Most rest in winter, bloom in spring, and shed what no longer serves them in autumn. There's no rush, only a natural unfolding.

As storytellers, we are part of this same ecosystem. Our creativity isn't diminished by rest, reflection, or slow growth. It thrives when we embrace our cyclical rhythm and recognize that our pauses are just as valuable as our blooms.

THE TRUTH: Creativity Ebbs & Flows

Spring's unfolding doesn't happen all at once. A garden in early spring is full of starts and stops. Some seeds sprout quickly. Others wait for the right moment. Some remain dormant, gathering strength beneath the soil.

This isn't failure — it's resilience. Nature's growth patterns are adaptive, responding to water, sunlight, temperature, and nutrients. Each element affects the others, creating an intricate, ever-changing balance. And we, as a part of nature, are no different.

Our creative cycles follow a similar rhythm. Some ideas bloom immediately, while others linger in the back of our minds. Some grow stronger with time, while others break down, nourishing new ideas in their place. The key is knowing that this cycle isn't a problem to solve — it's part of the process.

SPRING BRINGS CHANGE, NOT STEADY GROWTH

Our bodies are not obstacles to creativity. They are the ecosystem that makes it possible. Just like the soil needs to rest and draw in nutrients before each bloom, our creative pauses are fertile ground for our stories to grow. If an idea is worth germinating, our bodies will dedicate energy to move the idea out of our head and into the world.

When we struggle to find enough energy or attention, it's often because the idea is not ready to put our precious, limited resources toward. We must learn to listen inward, instead of resist.

Neurodivergent and disabled storytellers experience heightened sensory and emotional awareness. We sense creative changes long before they form into coherent stories. A smell, a sound, or a shift in someone's mood or tone might spark inspiration.

Our bodies often know before our minds do. This intuitive awareness, this body wisdom, is a strength we are naturally attuned to. Just as animals know when to migrate, our bodies guide us toward creative opportunities.

In spring, our senses are inundated with fresh sources of stimuli. A story seedling may stir when we hear birdsong or notice the first green buds on a tree. Maybe a character takes shape when we feel the warm sun of a spring afternoon on our faces.

Instead of avoiding or numbing these stimuli, we can learn to let them process without judgment. If an idea arrives, we can follow its lead. If inspiration wanes, we can rest without guilt. By trusting this cyclical nature, we create space for stories to emerge in their own time.

THE WISDOM OF EXPERIMENTAL APPROACHES

Experimental creativity requires us to accept uncertainty. Many storytellers try to force a system onto their creative process. Typical advice encourages us to figure out what kind of storyteller we are. But the truth is, not all stories form and grow in the same way. Just like each plant has its own needs and growing seasons, so do ideas.

While stories typically grow in the same progression — inspiration, prewriting, draft, editing, publication — the process for each area shifts depending on the project's needs and the resources we have available.

As neurodivergent brains and disabled bodies, we must learn to trust our body's wisdom. We have to approach storytelling with creative curiosity. Not to force the process, but to evaluate the resources and choose what best supports the story's growth.

This requires us to be okay with imperfect action. In our instantaneous world, we rarely get to see the messy work of fellow creatives. By studying historic storytellers, we learn much of their work never saw an audience beyond themselves. They kept journals, common books, and drawers full of half-written manuscripts filled with experimental work.

If we want to create unforgettable works, we must learn to approach storytelling with a similar experimental attitude. This requires us to abandon formulas, arbitrary goals, and any concern with constructing perfect narratives. Instead, we must begin each day with curiosity. If we show up willing to get our hands dirty and nurture our ideas, we will produce something beautiful.

It's also important to note that not all seedlings require planting in our creative gardens at the same time. We can germinate dozens of story ideas in the greenhouse of our notebooks or computers and decide when they are mature enough to transplant.

This is where trusting our inner wisdom comes into play. We must follow our brain and body's energetic lead. If we rush to put too much in the ground, we'll exhaust our resources and nothing will grow well. Likewise, only planting one story idea may never bear fruit because the pollinators of fellow writers and audience move on to stories that are in full bloom.

ENERGY REQUIREMENTS & CREATIVITY

In the chronic illness community, we often compare energy to spoons. Spoon theory says we wake up with a certain number of spoons in our drawer. Able-bodied, neurotypical individuals usually wake up with roughly the same number and enough to get them through their day. But we can wake up with too many to hold — anxiety. Or none at all — exhaustion.

Simple daily activities may require the use of more of our spoons than they would the average person. For instance, a shower may take two or three for us, while only taking one for them.

So when we have to choose how we spend our spoons, creativity often gets bumped to the bottom of the priority list. Even when we choose to use one, we can easily use that spoon to debate which project idea is "good enough."

Instead, we can honor our energy by asking ourselves, what best fits the resources we have in this season? What do we have the time to nourish and maintain?

If we're in a limited spoon season, perhaps we choose a story idea that is in a genre we read frequently and understand the readers' expectations of. Maybe we write a novella instead of a novel. Or a short story for an anthology, so we don't have to worry about learning publication right now. Maybe we choose something closer to our lived experience so we don't have to research an unfamiliar career or historical context.

If we find our resources increase, we can always add layers or finish a project early and start something new. But in this spring season of experimentation, the importance is to test out ideas that align with our energy and feel good in our mind and body. This will keep us from burning out and lead us to the work that will bear fruit.

Journal Reflection: What resources do you have available right now? How much time, energy, attention, and physical/mental space do you really have to give?

OUR LIBERATION: Moving Through Spring with Agency

Spring officially begins at the equinox — the point at which the days and nights are equal in length. This falls in late March in the northern hemisphere and late September in the southern hemisphere. However, many cultures use factors other than the sun to mark the beginning of spring.

Some celebrate spring when the rivers unfreeze or when the first flowers sprout through the hard earth. Others choose to celebrate when certain animals emerge from their dens.

There is no "right way" to denote spring's beginning. In reality, all these phenomena fall within the same few weeks. What is important is to follow our body's wisdom and be aware of the shift.

HONORING WINTER'S RESPITE & SPRING'S POTENTIAL

However you choose to mark spring, it's important to appreciate the liminal transition between seasons. This is a powerful phase that happens four times a year. As nature transitions, so do our bodies. There are plenty of shifts as we leave winter and enter spring. The weather changes, daylight lengthens, the earth warms, snow melts, and plants sprout. Even insects and animals come out of hibernation.

Our lives reflect these changes too. We change how we dress, how we warm or cool our homes, how much natural versus artificial light we use, how much time we spend outdoors, and what fresh foods we eat. But none of it is certain.

The early days of spring arrive with hesitation — frost lingering in morning shadows while new green pushes through soil still cold from winter. This natural tension mirrors our creative emergence after periods of dormancy. Many creative methodologies rush us into productivity, demanding us to blossom when our internal timing still requires gentle nurturing.

The transition from winter's introspection to spring's expansive potential creates a unique creative threshold. This liminal space deserves recognition as its own phase.

In early spring, our creative energy may fluctuate dramatically. One day, it may flow freely. The next, it might retreat into protective stillness. This rhythm isn't inconsistency, but a natural oscillation between what has been and what is becoming.

We can honor this tension by:

- Dedicating space for both reflection and creative practices.
- Allowing contradictory creative impulses to coexist.
- Documenting the feelings that arise as we transition.
- Resisting pressure to abandon winter's insights in favor of spring's actions.

Mainstream creative advice frames this tension as "resistance" or "creative block," pathologizing this natural transition. Instead, recognize this emergence as a delicate unfurling that cannot be rushed.

EARLY SPRING (EMERGENT PHASE): GENTLE PRACTICES FOR LOW-ENERGY DAYS

Early spring often brings energy fluctuations as our creative systems adjust to new growth. Rather than forcing these natural variations to be more uniform, we can develop practices that adapt to our changing capacity.

One way is to map your creative energy. Before beginning any writing session, assess your current energy on a scale of 1-5. Match what imperfect actions you want to take to your energy level. Create a personalized menu for your current projects of activities for each energy level.

Another option is to have threshold practices that require minimal energy but maintain a connection to your creative work. These might include gentle note-taking, collecting sensory impressions, or simply sitting with your project without pressure to produce.

For those with busy minds, shifting to a body-based creative practice and integrating movement may be helpful. Think about your project while on a slow walk. Engage in repetitive movements, like knitting or folding laundry while contemplating a creative question. Or use gestures or objects to explore concepts when words feel inaccessible.

And if you're in an extremely low-energy season, maybe even a negative spoon season, design a micro-creative session that feels complete in less than five minutes. Two great examples of this are six-word stories and one-photo-a-day storytelling. These need only brief flexes of your creative muscles, followed by a written note or photograph. If you're in a flare or recovering from a medical procedure, you might choose to keep a one-line-a-day creative journal or a quote journal of inspirational lines you read or hear in other people's work.

Remember that low-energy periods aren't creative failures but essential phases in your sovereign rhythm. Prioritize rest, but keep space for your creativity to show up.

MID-SPRING (VIBRANT PHASE): USING ENERGY BURSTS WITHOUT DRAINING OURSELVES

As spring fully arrives, the natural world enters a phase of vibrant expansion. Flowers bloom, birds nest with purpose, and the earth becomes a rainbow of color in a few short weeks. During this time, we hit the mid-point of spring — May 1st in the northern hemisphere and October 31st in the southern hemisphere. This day is often a celebration of creative energy.

Many neurodivergent and disabled storytellers mirror this energy in periods of intense creative inspiration that hits unexpectedly and demands expression. Mid-spring creative energy often manifests as powerful hyperfocus or manic productivity.

Now that nature has settled into a moderate temperature and stable weather, we feel our best and most clear-headed. These productive states allow us to create remarkable work but can lead to dangerous depletion. The challenge becomes not how to create more or faster, but how to create sustainably within these intense phases.

To do so, we must prepare self-care before entering deep work. Before our creative sessions, it's important to take time to design support systems for our future selves. These might be things like setting water or food break notifications, prepping recovery spaces for our bodies, and establishing gentle exit strategies like standing up and stretching so we can transition easily.

When in hyperfocus, external cues with gentle transitions are critical. They create containers with defined boundaries around intense creative sessions. These should not be arbitrary, like the Pomodoro method, but meaningful and aligned for you and your brain and body's needs.

For me, this looks like awakening all my senses and centering in the now with a 5-4-3-2-1 exercise before I begin my creative session. I identify five things I can see. Four things I can touch. Three things I can hear. Two things I can smell. And one thing I can taste, which is usually whatever I'm drinking during that session. This grounds me in the moment, and lets me show up fully present.

I set my timer for 45 minutes on a high energy day, less when I'm recovering from a migraine or just have other things that need my spoons later in the day. When that timer goes off, I save my work, stand up, and stretch. Then I turn on a song and take a snack or drink break. If I have more time, I'll repeat. If not, I'll move on to another task on my get-to-do list. If I'm recovering, I will close my computer, roll over in bed, and take a catnap before transitioning to my next task.

Whatever your session looks like, make sure to check in with your body regularly. Develop awareness of your sensory state during creative intensity. Make a personalized checklist of physical signals that indicate approaching depletion. For some, it may be eye strain. For others, it may be tension or an ache in a joint or muscle. Whatever your body signals are, establish non-negotiable self-care protocols.

And make sure to integrate post-creative recovery as part of your process. Frame recovery as essential rather than lost productivity time. Design specific practices that honor whatever is necessary to reintegrate after intense creation. Maybe for you, that is a 5-4-3-2-1 sensory check in to come back to the real world. If you have stiffness in your body or did a long sitting session, maybe it is a form of movement you enjoy. Or if you have chronic fatigue, it may be the ability to lie down or rest your head and close your eyes.

Mainstream creative advice often glorifies working through the night or besting yourself in multiple back-to-back sprints. Reject these harmful ideas by establishing practices that protect your well-being while honoring your unique creative intensity.

LATE SPRING (RIPENING PHASE): PREPARING FOR SUMMER WHILE PROTECTING OUR CREATIVE AUTONOMY

As spring transitions toward summer, the natural world shifts from explosive growth to steady development. Pollination leads to the formation of fruit, leaves reach full expansion, and the ecosystem settles into a rhythm of maturation. This phase brings creative challenges and opportunities.

Late-spring's generative energy makes you particularly vulnerable to creative exploitation — both external requests that drain your resources and internalized expectations that push you toward unsustainable productivity. To prevent both, it's important to know your core values and to use them to assess what you spend your time and energy on.

My core values are authentic beauty, creative curiosity, meaningful work, liberating love, and intentional community. Whenever an idea for a story pops into my head or someone asks me to take on a ghostwriting project or coach them, I evaluate the opportunity against my values.

If someone wants me to write an enemies-to-lovers romance about two rival gardeners in a reality TV show competition, I can make the story idea align with my values.

But what if the author isn't someone I want to build community with? What if they are someone who can't finish their own work and want to profit off someone else's time and energy? This detracts from my projects and brand development. That conflicts with my inner desire to focus on meaningful work. Suddenly, the project is significantly less appealing.

When we have limited resources using our values to choose our projects or shifting our projects to align better with our values can be the difference between building a garden we can look back on in ten years and be amazed, or having a few beauties we're struggling to keep alive among a bed of weeds while gardens we helped others build blossom.

Along the vein of others' work versus our own, we also need to recognize exploitation. This may not be coaching or helping with an entire project. It may be as simple as participating in writing or critique groups where you spend more time giving advice and feedback than you receive. It might also be a particular person in your writing community who uses your brain as a crutch for their own lack of decisiveness or self-trust.

Whatever the reason, if someone is constantly using your spoons, you must create boundaries around that relationship. Remember that boundaries affect *your actions*, not theirs. What will you do when you encounter these situations? Having scripts for how you will handle these situations can be a game changer.

One boundary I have is I must be doing my own creative sessions regularly before I'll commit to taking on anyone else's work. If I'm neglecting my own, I don't have the spoons for someone else, and that is what I tell them. "Your project sounds interesting..." or "I'd love to help you figure this out..." and then I say, "...but right now I don't have the time or energy to work on my own stories, much less to be any help to someone else." This is polite but a firm no.

If I can check the resource box, but I am in a groove or on a personal deadline, I set a boundary that I will offer my assistance *after* I complete what I'm working on. If they just want quick advice, I'll give it at the end of my day if I still have the spoons. If they want more than a few minutes, I'll tell them I'd love to help, but it will have to be after I finish editing, drafting, etc. If they are willing to wait, I write on my calendar to check back in with them.

There will be times when someone can't respect our boundaries. If this happens, it's important to figure out how to end that relationship. This may sound severe, but people who don't respect boundaries will never reciprocate a healthy professional relationship.

Creating personal networking standards about the type of people and groups you will collaborate and work with is key. This isn't just ethics and values, although those are important. These are situations you know are problematic for you.

For example, I won't coach someone who isn't committed to finishing a project. Many first-time authors hop from idea to idea, looking for that dopamine fix. But they don't want to put in the work to complete all the phases to finish their project. These clients end up stalled and on my calendar for years coming back because they like working with me, but never making progress.

I also don't join communities that focus on arbitrary goals. This is where I started, and I'm grateful for all I learned, but word counts and set times or trying to finish a project in three, six, or twelve months doesn't work for me.

Thus, giving advice to storytellers who are working in those constrictions won't be authentic or make me feel joy.

Pocket Note: *Your creative energy is a precious resource. It deserves fierce protection. It's not a commodity to be extracted until you're depleted.*

CHAPTER 3: Creating on Our Own Terms

"Spring is the time of plans and projects." — *Leo Tolstoy*

THE MYTH: A Creative Schedule is Essential

Almost all craft books, courses, and conferences mention the necessity of a creative routine. Some experts recommend working at the same hour every day. Others accommodate full-time workers or caregivers with a suggestion to aim for a minimal number of words each day or a higher goal several days a week.

Even our fellow famous authors, playwrights, and creatives insist we put our creative time on our calendars. They reinforce the message that if we want to be "serious" storytellers, we need a disciplined routine.

This advice makes creativity another task on our never-ending to-do lists. And thanks to our productivity-centric society, we're encouraged to complete our "real work" first. Since there will always be more laundry, dishes, emails, and work assignments, we end up never getting to our creative projects, or coming to them exhausted.

But what if we acknowledge our brain doesn't work that way? What happens when we admit our body's capabilities change day to day? For those of us with neurodivergent minds and disabled bodies, these rigid expectations of productivity aren't just unhelpful — they're impossible to meet.

WHY INFLEXIBLE ROUTINES DON'T WORK FOR EVERYONE

Typical creative schedule advice assumes:
- Our energy levels are predictable.
- Our attention can focus on the task at hand easily.
- We can control our timetables and availability.

- Our body can handle the same demands consistently.

For most creatives, these are true. If they get sick or busy, they can still willpower through, forgoing other necessary activities, like eating or sleeping from time to time.

But for neurodivergent and disabled storytellers, these assumptions fall apart quickly. ADHD brains might hyperfocus intensely one day, yet struggle to even start the next. Autistic storytellers may need different sensory environments depending on their regulation state. Chronically ill creators may have days where sitting at a desk is physically impossible or episodes where their pain threshold is so high they cannot focus.

An AuDHD writer with fibromyalgia, I coached, tried for years to maintain an early morning writing schedule because that's what her favorite author recommended. She could achieve it from time to time, but most days she'd wake up late or be too tired to get into the headspace to work. Only after we explored this together, and I posed these questions, did she begin to listen to her body and pay attention to when her brain was most creative. Suddenly her desire to create shot back up, and she was finding pockets of time to be her most creative self. What she thought was a self-discipline problem was actually unachievable expectations.

HOW SCHEDULES IGNORE OUR RHYTHMS

Standard creative advice rarely accounts for our diverse needs. Nor does it account for our natural creative cycles. Many of us don't create in neat, daily parcels of time, but rather in intense bursts followed by periods of rest to refuel our inspiration and play with ideas.

As mentioned earlier, many storytelling experts do not consider that some of us struggle with executive functions, like task initiation and prioritizing projects. Many of us also have unique sensory needs. Even things like what medications we take can impact when or if we can work.

Traditional schedules also ignore the natural creativity cycles many people with diverse minds and rebellious bodies experience. Sometimes I may not write for two weeks, then suddenly pen twenty thousand words in three days. That is how my brain works. Other storytellers who struggle with illnesses or disabilities can only work on their projects when they're having periods of wellness. Then they require seasons of rest to focus on self-care when they are in an active flare or undergoing medical procedures.

THE SHAME-BASED COMPULSION TO PUSH BEYOND OUR LIMITS

Perhaps the most harmful myth is that we should push through discomfort to maintain our creative schedules.

We're told that discipline means ignoring our body's stress signals, or that commitment means working despite pain or exhaustion.

This advice doesn't just ignore our needs — it actively harms us. It creates a cycle of shame where we blame ourselves for not meeting these impossible standards. It teaches us to distrust our bodies and brains. And it usually leads to creative burnout, physical injury, and worsening health conditions.

Worst of all, shame becomes part of the story we tell ourselves. The message that plays on repeat is that "real storytellers" follow rigid schedules regardless of their circumstances. But insisting on conformity is internalized *ableism* — the belief that only people capable of normal function have value. It assumes we live in a world where everyone has equal ability.

But we don't.

When we try to keep rigid timetables, we set ourselves up for a painful relationship with our creativity. We begin to see our natural rhythms as character flaws rather than valid ways of being. This causes us to devalue rest, self-care, and acceptance of our disability or our need for more resources to take the same action.

THE TRUTH: Our Capacity Changes Every Day

The reality for many neurodivergent and disabled storytellers is that our capacity isn't static. It changes, sometimes dramatically, from one day to the next. This isn't a weakness or a lack of discipline. It's simply how our brains and bodies work.

THE DIFFERENCE BETWEEN HYPERFOCUS & SUSTAINED ENERGY

One of the trickiest aspects of divergent brains and disabled bodies is distinguishing between two very different energy states: hyperfocus and sustained energy.

Hyperfocus is especially common with ADHD and Autism, but also happens for those with conditions such as fibromyalgia and MS. These periods when our minds and bodies align, allowing us to take decisive action, can feel like a creative superpower. Hours pass in what feels like minutes. Stories flow effortlessly. Ideas connect in exciting ways.

But hyperfocus is rarely sustainable. It comes at a cost — depleting our energy reserves and leading to the need for longer recovery. This is because, while we are capable of attentive productivity during those hours, we neglect our regular needs. Sometimes this happens out of fear we won't feel this energetic again. Sometimes, we ignore our body's signals out of sheer focus, missing cues to eat, sleep, or take our meds.

Sustained energy, on the other hand, might feel less exciting but allows for more consistent creative practice without crashing. It respects our physical, mental, and emotional limits and leaves margins for rest. Ideally, we schedule in rest and self-care as well as space for all our functional needs into our schedule before and after our creative window. We leave our work feeling anticipation for our next session, not exhaustion.

Learning to tell the difference between these states is crucial.

It helps to ask ourselves:

- How does my body feel during this creative session?
- Did I remember to eat, drink, and take breaks?
- How will I likely feel when this energy ends?
- Can I stop when I need to? Or does the work feel compulsive?

Our unique energy patterns spiral through cycles of ability and disability. Understanding this helps us make better decisions about how to enjoy the ease of hyperfocus with healthy limits. More importantly, it allows us to rely on more sustainable practices the other 90% of our time.

HOW SPRING'S CLIMATE AFFECTS US

For many divergent brains and disabled bodies, external factors like weather and environment profoundly affect our creative capacity.

As mentioned earlier, weather sensitivity is real. Changes in barometric pressure can trigger migraines or joint pain. Humidity can worsen certain conditions. Seasonal light shifts can affect mood and energy levels. Rather than ignoring these factors, we must acknowledge them as legitimate influences on our creative capacity.

Our physical environment also shapes what's creatively possible. Noise, light, temperature, and seating can make the difference between a productive session and a difficult one. Many of us need alternative environmental setups depending on our sensory needs and pain levels each day.

Tracking these patterns can help us work with rather than against our bodies. It's important to notice which weather conditions affect our creativity. Many of us find a color-based or rating-based habit tracker useful in recording these factors. Comparing them over time, we can see how different factors support or hinder our work. If we have a singular issue like migraines, we can also keep two lists — one for easy days and one for tough days — and record what sensory issues impact are in play.

WHY CREATIVE SPACES NEED TO WORK FOR OUR BRAINS & BODIES

Traditional creative spaces often contain things like LED lights and straight-backed chairs designed for neurotypical, able bodies. They assume a certain posture, a certain way of focusing, a certain relationship with sensory input.

But our brains and bodies have different needs. We may focus better when moving, lying down, or with specific accommodations. Our pain levels might require positions that look "unprofessional" but allow us to create comfortably.

The truth is, the right creative space is the one that works for our individual needs on any given day.

This might mean:
- Multiple options for seating or positioning.
- Alternate lighting options for different sensory needs.
- Tools for managing sound like headphones, white noise, etc.
- Textures or weighted items that provide comfort or sensory regulation.
- Accessibility tools that reduce physical strain.

When we create spaces that accommodate our needs, we remove unnecessary barriers to our creativity. We stop wasting energy fighting our environments and redirect that energy toward our creative work.

Journal Reflection: What is one thing you could add and one thing you could eliminate from your preferred creative space to help you work with more ease?

OUR LIBERATION: Designing Our Creative Space

Freedom comes when we stop forcing ourselves into environments that weren't designed for us. Instead, we can create systems and spaces that honor our unique needs and capacities.

COMFORTABLE SPACES FOR SUSTAINABLE CREATIVITY

Designing a space that truly works for us means challenging conventional ideas about what a proper workspace looks like. Throw away the idea of a perfect storyteller's space and listen to your body.

Do you really work better in one specific space? Do you work better sitting? Lying reclined? Pacing while you work out ideas? Writing at a coffee shop? Acting out your scenes? Hand drawing storyboards? Or working on a tablet?

If you aren't imagining one vivid way of working that lights you up and is always available, consider creating multiple creative stations.

It may be helpful to have a conventional desk setup for certain types of work, like writing emails to our audience. But consider the height, workspace, and what kind of chair, and lighting you need. Do you require back support, a footrest, or an ergonomic keyboard? What smells, sounds, and visual inputs do you need to add or eliminate? What tasks will you do there? How long can you work there comfortably?

You should also have a comfortable chair or couch for days when you need more support, like when editing, and you need your brain more than your body. For high pain days, reclined in bed using a portable device can be essential.

While these are what we navigate toward first, it is really important that we be able to work on the go or while standing or walking, inside and outside, so that we don't get too sedentary or limited in movement, unless that is the nature of our conditions.

Stock these spaces with tools that reduce friction. You may want easy-to-use recording devices or apps on your phone, tablet, or computer for days when writing is difficult. Comfortable pens and paper that don't cause muscle strain. Dictation software for verbal processing. Sensory tools and toys that help with regulation.

Think about environmental factors:
- Lighting options for different sensory needs.
- Temperature control (extra blankets, fans, etc.)
- Sound management (headphones, white noise machines)

- Scent options that help with focus or comfort.

The goal isn't to create an Instagram-worthy creative space, but one that truly supports your needs and makes creativity more accessible.

DESIGN ADAPTIVE INSPIRATION CAPTURE TECHNOLOGY

How we feel mentally, emotionally, or physically can impact our desire to use a tool. When I'm lying in bed with a migraine, I don't want to handwrite notes or look at a bright screen. I just want to hit a button and leave a message.

Curate an alternate method for capturing your ideas and words for your high pain or worst brain fog days.

If you have dyslexia or dysgraphia, you may prefer to dictate because it's more accurate and easier to have read back to you. Or you might choose to use multiple apps based on how you feel. When you're over-stimulated or scattered, an assistive AI app can help you generate or streamline an idea. But on another day, a digital whiteboard can allow you to work with a writing partner. Likewise, you may choose a cute glittery notebook for rough days just because it makes you happy and gives you a dopamine boost.

Consider shortcuts for brain fog moments. For example, if your stories have technical or historical details, you might type *(INSERT)* into your manuscript and add research later.

Or, if you're a visual storyteller using video or images, you might use a template or a placeholder for content. If you use a stylus on a tablet, you can create gestural or single-touch shortcuts to program words or phrases you have trouble with. Or use a framework for how you write emails or blog posts.

Another helpful tool is cross-platform synchronization, which doesn't require manual transfers or complex workflows. If you like to use a transcriber app and work in a word processor program, consider using their in-app transcriber feature. Most programs now have in-app options. Or you can pick one that integrates automatically.

Also remember, new options come out every month. Research integrative and adaptive technologies for your specific sensory and accommodation needs.

BRINGING NATURE INTO WORKSPACES

Connecting with nature benefits creativity. But traditional advice to "take a walk" or "sit in the park" isn't always accessible. Instead, we can bring elements of nature into our creative spaces.

Consider:
- Positioning workspaces near windows with natural light.

- Using plants that require minimal care but provide sensory benefits.
- Creating a "nature box" with collected items for tactile connection.
- Using nature sounds or videos when actual outdoor time isn't possible.
- Incorporating natural scents that bring you joy.

Even small connections to nature can shift our creative energy and provide sensory experiences that support our work.

PRACTICE: CREATIVE SPACE AUDIT

While typical advice encourages us to focus on the external form and function of our space, we can reject these by listening to our bodies and prioritizing accessibility and flexibility.

Evaluate your current creative space with these essential questions:

- Does it accommodate my physical needs?
- Does it support my sensory requirements?
- Can I adapt it to different energy levels?
- Does it reduce or add to my executive function load?
- Does it bring me joy or just follow conventional expectations?

Consider these changes:

- Lighting control that honors visual needs, like adjustable levels, indirect lighting, and non-fluorescent options.
- Sound management like noise-canceling headphones, white noise, and acoustic dampening.
- Temperature regulation tools like cooling vests, heating pads, and adjustable layers.
- Comfort objects to provide proprioceptive feedback like weighted blankets, balance boards, and resistance bands.
- Scent enhancers or neutralizers like scented candles, oil diffusers, air purifiers, and ozone machines.
- Aesthetics that fit cognitive processing demands like dopamine decorating or minimalism to limit distractions.
- Writing tools requiring minimal sensory negotiation like smooth pens/pencils, quality paper, devices in dark mode, quiet choices, etc.
- Organizational systems that align with your thinking and work patterns like color/size order, labels, or placing all items used in view and within reach.
- Clear boundaries to establish work mode like closed doors, time limits, and communication signals.

Elements for the neurodivergent brain:

- Add visual cues for routine actions that reduce decision fatigue.
- Incorporate technology that bridges executive function gaps such as planning apps.
- Plan for time blindness with gentle reminders and margins rather than rigid deadlines.
- Arrange reference materials for minimal cognitive load.
- Creating workflows that can be paused and resumed with minimal effort.

Elements for the chronically ill or disabled:

- Multiple working positions, such as sitting, standing, or reclining.
- Ergonomic supports specific to your body's needs.
- Eating, hydrating, and medication routines that don't require additional mental effort.
- Rest zones that allow for quick breaks without losing creative momentum.
- Pain management tools within easy reach.

Pocket Note: *Your workspace can serve as both sanctuary and studio. Calibrate your space for your exact needs, allowing creativity to continue even during challenging sensory periods. This won't just produce better work. It will honor your whole self as a storyteller. You are worthy of accommodation and care.*

CHAPTER 4: Embodying Our Stories

"Create whatever causes a revolution in your heart. The rest of it will take care of itself." — Elizabeth Gilbert

THE MYTH: Creativity is a Mental Activity

For generations, we've been fed the persistent myth that creativity is purely intellectual. As a mystical spark of the mind, our inspiration and ability to form story are disconnected from our physical existence. This myth has shaped how we talk about, teach, and value creative work, often to our detriment.

THE FALSE SEPARATION BETWEEN MIND & BODY

This myth of the disembodied creative mind pervades our culture. We speak of "brainstorming" but never "body-storming." We celebrate the genius of intellect while overlooking the wisdom of our physical selves. The advice we receive reflects this false separation—clear our mind, focus harder, and push through creative blocks.

This mind-body dualism has dominated Western thought for centuries. It insists that the mind, which is supposedly rational and disciplined, must control and overcome the physical, which is emotional and limiting. In creative practice, this translates to a hierarchy where thinking overrides feeling. Where pushing through physical discomfort is noble. Where the body's signals are treated as distractions rather than vital information.

COMMON ADVICE IGNORES THE BODY'S ROLE

These instructions treat our bodies as mere vessels — sometimes troublesome ones — that transport our brains. When fatigue sets in, we're told to power through. When our backs ache from hours of sitting, we're advised to ignore it in the service of the work. When seasonal depression dampens our creative fire, we're encouraged to force productivity anyway.

This advice presumes our bodies operate like machines, with consistent energy levels, minimal sensory processing needs, and no physical limitations. It treats variation in physical capacity as weakness or lack of discipline rather than natural human diversity.

WHY PUSHING THROUGH PAIN DOESN'T WORK

"No pain, no gain" might work for fictional sports movies, but it's disastrous for sustainable creative practice.

When we repeatedly override our body's signals, our nervous system enters a state of persistent threat and vigilance. It floods us with adrenaline and cortisol to fight or flee, even though we are not in actual danger.

Our creative capacity actually diminishes as survival mechanisms take the lead. We act according to our historic patterns of trauma response. For some, that may look like hacking away at a project with perfectionistic tendencies that lead to no actual progress — fighting. Others will stay busy with everything but their work — fleeing. Still others, it may take the form of disassociation, where they are constantly thinking about their project but can't engage in it — freezing.

Historically, we've developed false associations between creative work and suffering. Whether it is the starving artist, the mentally anguished, tortured artist, or the compulsive creator, we all have negative stories that play through our heads about how crafting story must cost us something, and it is often our physical well-being.

The "tortured artist" archetype glamorizes this disconnection, treating burnout, addiction, and self-destruction as necessary prices for successful art — when in fact, these are consequences of ignoring our embodied needs, not prerequisites for brilliance.

HOW ABLEISM IS WOVEN INTO CREATIVE ADVICE

This mind-centric approach to creativity isn't just incomplete, it's harmful. It's rooted in ableist assumptions that everyone's body functions the same way, that physical limitations are mere obstacles to overcome rather than integral parts of our creative identities. It leaves no room for the creator with chronic pain, the storyteller with sensory processing differences, or the artist whose energy ebbs and flows with invisible rhythms.

These barriers systematically exclude disabled, chronically ill, and neurodivergent creators from mainstream production and recognition. They send a clear message that "true artists" don't have limits. But all bodies have limits. Some of us simply can't ignore ours.

It's no wonder that we live in our heads when we spend our creative energy justifying our existence and proving our worth is more than just the ability to produce fresh stories. This often leads to dependence on substances like caffeine and sugar to create artificial energy to engage our work, even though their use costs us later.

THE TRUTH: Our Bodies Birth Our Stories

Our body isn't separate from our creativity. It's the birthplace of it.

What if we've had it backward all along? What if the body isn't an obstacle to creative work but its very source? What if physical sensations, rhythms, and needs aren't distractions from creativity but essential guidance systems for it? What if the brain is only one part of an integrated whole and most storytellers have ignored 80% of their creative potential?

DIVERSE BRAINS & BODIES OFFER UNIQUE PERSPECTIVES

Every story we tell, every character we create, every world we build emerges not just from our thoughts but from our embodied experience. We each have our own distinctive neurological wiring, our particular sensory perceptions, and unique ways our body moves through space. These aren't distractions from creative work, but the very foundations of it.

Consider how diverse bodies and brains create diverse stories. The author with synesthesia, who perceives sounds as colors, brings a different palette to their work than the writer who doesn't. The storyteller who navigates the world with chronic pain understands conflict and resolution in ways others might not. The creator whose attention shifts and flows uncontrollably may discover surprising connections between seemingly unrelated ideas.

Our creative work emerges not despite our bodies but through them — through the specific ways we perceive, process, and interact with the world.

These aren't deficits to overcome, but truth signals that generate distinct creative perspectives. Our particular bodies and brains don't limit our stories. They are the very conditions that make our specific artistic contributions possible. No one else can produce what we can create because no one else experiences the world through our unique bodies.

THE WAY SEASONAL CHANGES AFFECT OUR CREATIVITY

Our bodies exist in constant dialogue with natural

cycles. The light-dark patterns of days and seasons affect our hormones, energy levels, and neurochemistry. These aren't irrelevant biological facts. They're the rhythmic foundation of our creative capacity.

Our bodies attune us to the natural world in ways our conscious minds often miss. The seasonal shifts that affect our energy, mood, and focus aren't inconveniences to overcome. They're creative guidance systems. Winter's inward pull isn't a creative block but an invitation to gestate ideas in darkness. Summer's expansive energy isn't a distraction but a time for exploration and play.

Rather than fighting these cycles with artificial consistency, we can work with them, allowing different phases of projects to align with our natural energetic seasons. This isn't giving in to limitations. It's strategic alignment with our biological rhythms.

UNDERSTANDING OUR BODY'S WISDOM AS ARTISTIC GUIDANCE

What we call "writer's block" or "creative resistance" often isn't psychological at all. It's physical intelligence at work. Restlessness may be our body telling us that our project needs movement, play, or a different approach. Fatigue may suggest our work requires rest, integration time, or less force. Tension in our neck or chest may signal misalignment with our authentic voice.

These sensations aren't random noise or inconvenient distractions. They're sophisticated information systems evolved over millennia to guide our actions. What if we trusted them as much as our intellectual analysis?

REFRAMING SYMPTOMS AS SIGNALS OF OUR NEEDS

For those with chronic conditions, symptoms aren't just obstacles, they're communications. Pain, fatigue, brain fog, and sensory sensitivity aren't random malfunctions, but meaningful signals about our needs and boundaries. When we reframe symptoms as messengers rather than enemies, we can learn to listen with compassion to our bodies.

One of the first things I noticed when I started listening to my body was that I would migraine when I forced myself into external expectations. My body was demanding a gentler approach. This led to changes in where I worked, how I worked, and for how long.

My brain fog from migraines and the associated medications made working difficult. But once I started listening to my body, and stopped forcing my brain to function when it needed rest, I found the fog lifted. I discovered I could engage in certain cognitive processes, like meditation.

I use brain fog as a tool now. Because while it obscures so much, what still presses through is something my body needs me to pay attention to. Likewise, my heightened sensitivity to smells, noise, and textures while I migraine helps me refine my environment to better support my needs.

These shifts transformed my relationship with my body from adversarial to collaborative. Rather than working despite my physical pain, I learned to work in partnership with it, interpreting the signals my body sends as valuable creative direction.

Journal Reflection: *What is one "symptom" you frequently experience while creating story? What could it be telling you about your creative process?*

OUR LIBERATION: Body-Friendly Creative Practices

Freeing our creativity from the mind-body split doesn't mean abandoning discipline or structure. Rather, it means creating practices that work with our body's wisdom instead of against it.

TECHNIQUES TO WORK WITH OUR BODY

Body-friendly creativity begins with practices that honor rather than override our physical experience.

Try some of these techniques.

- **Body-storming (embodied brainstorming)**: As the weather turns nicer, go for a walk or move your body in a free-form way and listen for the story inside you. Express those ideas out loud and record them with a transcription app. When stuck on a scene, embody your characters—how would they stand, move, and breathe?
- **Sensory awareness**: Notice which sensory details in your environment support your best thinking. Experiment with the scents and the sounds of spring to find fresh additions.
- **Rhythm matching**: Align different creative tasks with your physical energy patterns. When you are restless, get up and move or do housework with a digital recorder to capture your ideas. When you're tired, listen to a podcast or audiobook or watch a show or movie in a similar setting, with a similar character, theme, or genre to wind down.
- **Permission to pause**: Before and after your creative work sessions, check in with your body. Do you need to hydrate, eat, use the bathroom, rest, or move? Also, notice how your body feels. Is there tension or discomfort? Consider ways you can alleviate strain in the future. What is that sensation telling you about your work? Perhaps you're holding on too tightly to how you think the story should go. Or maybe you're tiptoeing around the real meat of

the story because you're afraid to delve into something that might be controversial.

These approaches recognize that creativity doesn't just happen in our heads — it emerges through our entire physical being. When we engage our whole selves, our work becomes not just more sustainable but richer and more authentic.

WAYS TO CREATE WHILE MANAGING PAIN & FATIGUE

Chronic pain and fatigue don't have to mean creative hibernation. With thoughtful adaptations, creation remains possible even during difficult physical periods.

- **Micro-dosing creativity:** Commit to ten-minute creative sessions (or less) that respect your energy boundaries.
- **Dictation and transcriptions:** Capture your ideas without the physical demands of writing.
- **Work-rest balance:** Deliberately plan recovery time after creative sessions.
- **Medium switching**: Shift between handwriting, typing, and speaking as your capacity allows.
- **Pain-conscious positioning**: Work in positions that minimize pain.

These strategies acknowledge pain and fatigue as real while preventing them from becoming barriers to expression. The goal isn't to ignore our limits but to work within them.

SIMPLE BREATHING & MOVEMENT TO SUPPORT CREATIVITY

Our breath and basic movements powerfully influence our nervous system state. This directly impacts creative capacity. Simple somatic practices can help shift from stress responses to a balanced state where creativity thrives.

Box breathing is easy. Picture a box. Each side is a step of breathing — inhale, hold, exhale, hold. Count to four as you slide along each side of the square. This breath exercise regulates the nervous system, activating a calm response where creativity occurs.

Another useful tool is gentle stretches of the spine and neck. Because we often stay in the same posture for an extended period, our muscles get stiff. Simply lifting our chin toward the ceiling, then lowering toward our chest as we slowly inhale and exhale can strengthen and relax those supportive muscles. You can also turn your head side to side or gently lower each ear toward your shoulder. None of this should cause pain, only a gentle stretch. If you have pain, consider seeking some professional physical therapy or medical guidance.

Another technique I use frequently is progressive facial relaxation. Start by opening your jaw, so your teeth aren't touching. Then lower your tongue from the roof of your mouth. Gently shift your lower jaw side to side until you feel the release.

Then take hold of your ears and gently rotate them a few times. If you yawn, that is a positive signal that your nervous system is relaxing. Stroke along your cheekbones with your thumbs, then along your nose, before moving up to just above your eyebrows.

Let your eyes peer left, then right for as long as you can tolerate. Then gaze upward and downward without moving your chin. Close your eyes. Take a nice deep breath and notice how much more relaxed you feel.

The third technique I find useful is simply crossing my arms and tapping the opposite side of my body. This *bilateral stimulation* is easy to do even around others in a coffee shop.

Tap each thigh with the opposite hand, or hug yourself and tap along your ribcage. You can do the same along each upper arm or shoulder. You can tap both sides simultaneously to create energy or alternate to calm your system. Use whatever tempo works for you.

These aren't esoteric practices. They're practical tools that realign our physiological state with our creative intentions, making flow states more accessible even when we're facing challenges. If you find any of them useful, you can explore them further by seeking out an expert in the technique.

PRACTICE: GROUNDING EXERCISES FOR SENSORY OVERLOAD

For many neurodivergent storytellers, sensory overload can disrupt creative flow. Practical grounding techniques can help restore balance when sensory processing becomes overwhelming.

- **5-4-3-2-1 technique**: Naming five things you see, four you feel, three you hear, two you smell, and one you taste. This exercise will ground you in your current environment when your brain is moving too fast, or you feel disconnected from the real world.
- **Weighted sensations**: Using weighted blankets, lap pads, or gentle pressure helps to restore sensory regulation. You can also use a weighted eye mask or lift something semi-heavy with your hands or feet like a thick book to give that resistance that allows your body to feel safe and in control.
- **Humming or singing:** Vocal vibration soothes the vagus nerve and nervous system. Use this anytime you feel your chest is tight or anxiety is building.
- **Cold water immersion:** Brief exposure to cold water on your face, hands, or wrists can reset sensory processing.

These techniques offer practical ways to return to

creative work when sensory experiences become overwhelming, allowing us to navigate challenges without abandoning our expression entirely.

When we liberate creativity from purely mental models and return it to the body, we discover not limitation but expansion. Our physical experiences — including pain, fatigue, sensitivity, and natural rhythms — aren't obstacles to creativity but sources of unique insight, authentic expression, and sustainable practice. By freeing stories to flow through our entire being, we create work that resonates with truth precisely because it emerges from our whole embodied selves.

Remember that creativity isn't just in our minds, it's in our fingers typing, our lungs breathing, and our hearts beating. It's in the way our eyes perceive color and light, the way our ears catch rhythm and cadence. It's in our body's memories and instincts. It's in our pleasure and pain.

Our creativity doesn't need to be forced through an uncooperative body. It needs to be welcomed, invited to flow through the perfectly imperfect vessel that is us. When we honor our physical self as an integral part of our creative identity, we'll find that our stories don't just come from us — they come through us, carried on the current of our embodied wisdom.

Pocket Note: *The most profound creative liberation comes not from transcending our bodies but from fully inhabiting* *them, allowing our stories to emerge from the rich, messy, beautiful experience of being human in all its complexity.*

CHAPTER 5: Freeing Up Energy and Attention

"In the spring, at the end of the day, you should smell like dirt. It's a reminder to be present and appreciate the simple things." — Margaret Atwood

THE MYTH: Our Attention Should be Focused

GREAT STORIES ONLY FORM DURING

FLOW STATE

The modern productivity culture tells us that success comes from cramming more activities into smaller time blocks. Terms like "Deep work," "flow state," and "laser focus" are presented as the gold standards of attention. While the concepts sound impressive, they often become weapons of self-criticism for those of us whose brains work differently. We're told that if we could just eliminate distractions and maintain unwavering concentration, we'd finally unlock our creative potential.

This myth is particularly dangerous because it suggests there's a direct correlation between attentive concentration and creative value. It implies that the more singularly focused we are, the better our stories will be. But this assumption dismisses the rich and complex ways neurodivergent minds and disabled bodies process information and generate ideas.

TYPICAL ADVICE IGNORES ATTENTION DIFFERENCES

Much of the advice we're given says all that stands in our way to having constant flow is distractions and uninterrupted time. But this assumes a neurotypical baseline for attention — one that simply doesn't apply to storytellers like us. This idea doesn't account for sensory processing differences, executive function variations, chronic pain, or fatigue that fluctuates throughout the day. Nor the fact that some brains are wired to make connections by gathering diverse inputs rather than shutting them out.

Some of us navigate neurological differences that affect how our focus works. Others balance chronic illnesses that create constant physical distractions. Many juggle caretaking responsibilities that drain mental and emotional attention before we even start our own work. Yet our productivity-centered society continues selling us the idea that if we just found the right routine or time-blocking technique, eliminated distractions, we'd overcome these "excuses."

THE HARMFUL LABELS OF "LAZY" VERSUS "DISCIPLINED"

Perhaps the most damaging aspect of the focused attention myth is how quickly it transforms into moral judgment. Those who maintain conventional focus get labeled disciplined, dedicated, or hardworking. Those who can't are dismissed as lazy, uncommitted, or lacking willpower.

These labels ignore neurological reality. What looks like distraction might actually be our brains making valuable connections. What appears as inconsistency could be our minds' natural rhythms for gathering and processing information. What seems like procrastination might be our systems' necessary preparation period before creative expression becomes possible.

The lazy/disciplined binary not only harms self-esteem, it misunderstands how diverse brains create. By internalizing these labels, we cut ourselves off from the very cognitive processes that make our stories exceptional.

THE TRUTH: We're Pattern & Relationship Creators

OUR SENSES TAKE IN MORE THAN MOST STORYTELLERS

Many neurodivergent and disabled storytellers experience the world with heightened sensory awareness. We notice sounds others filter out, feel sensations others never register, or detect patterns others overlook. This isn't a deficit. It's a different way of gathering information that translates into richly layered stories.

The autistic writer who notices minute details in conversation might create dialogue with subtle, realistic undertones. The person with chronic pain who's learned to interpret different bodily sensations might bring nuanced physical awareness to their characters. The ADHD creator whose attention shifts between foreground and background might capture environmental details that create immersive worlds.

Our stories often feel vivid precisely because we don't filter information the way others do. What looks like distraction is actually a different kind of attention — one that gathers more materials for our creative work.

OUR BRAINS REQUIRE INPUTS TO WORK WITH

Rather than starting with a blank page and generating ideas through linear focus, neurodivergent and disabled storytellers like us thrive on collecting and connecting diverse inputs. Our creative process often looks more like gathering interesting objects, conversations, sensations, and ideas, and then discovering the connections between them.

This isn't unfocused, it's differently focused. It's attention that spreads wide before going deep, that samples broadly before synthesizing. It's the recognition that our brains need raw materials to work with. Collecting these materials is a legitimate and necessary part of our creative process.

When we honor this need for story ingredients, we stop forcing ourselves into work methods that don't serve us. We recognize that scrolling through images, reading unrelated articles, or taking meandering walks may be exactly what our creative brains need to build connections that ultimately become our stories.

SAFE PLACE TO CURATE & EXPERIMENT WITH STORY IDEAS

For many neurodivergent, chronically ill, and disabled storytellers, the transition from collecting content to crafting stories requires a safe psychological space free from internalized judgment about how attention "should" work. We need permission to experiment with ideas without immediately evaluating their worth or worrying about how off-task they might appear.

This safe space may be a physical room where we can control sensory inputs. It could be a digital app like mind-mapping or a whiteboard that allows a non-linear collection of ideas. Or it may simply be the self-permission to follow seemingly random connections. Whatever form it takes, this space allows us to see patterns emerging from what might appear like chaos to others.

When we create these safe spaces for experimental play with concepts, characters, and sensations, we stop fighting our natural cognitive processes and start leveraging them. The result isn't just better stories, it's a more sustainable and joyful creative practice.

Journal Reflection: *Where in your home or community do you create your best stories? What elements do you need in order to feel focused and comfortable to create?*

OUR LIBERATION: Redefining What We Can Create

WANDERING FOCUS AS A PATHWAY TO STORY

What if the ebbs and flows of your concentration aren't obstacles to storytelling but essential components of it? What if the periods of scattered attention are gathering phases, and the periods of hyperfocus are synthesis phases? What if both are equally valuable?

Liberation comes when we stop seeing our wandering focus as something to overcome and start recognizing it as something to harness. The days when our attention seems to bounce between topics might be perfect for generating characters or settings. The days when we can concentrate deeply may be ideal for refining dialogue or structure.

By mapping our natural attention patterns and aligning our creative tasks with them, rather than resisting them, we can transform what most consider a limitation into a strength. Our stories will emerge not despite our wandering focus, but because of it.

HYPERFOCUS, MONOTROPISM, & OTHER ATTENTION PATTERNS

Mostly, when we talk about how neurodivergent and disabled storytellers focus, we discuss how split our attention is and how difficult it is to initiate tasks. But we can also hyperfocus on a task or subject or to redirect our attention into imaginary worlds easier than the average writer.

Neurodivergent creators with ADHD experience periods of hyperfocus more frequently than most people. Hyperfocus is an intense concentration on one task that excludes everything else. We may not get up for hours to eat, hydrate, move, or use the bathroom. Often, we don't even hear people around us. For storytellers, this can look like an intense research, planning, writing, or editing session that stretches across several hours.

Autistic storytellers may also experience a similar phenomenon called monotropism. This tendency keeps their focus intensely on one subject across days, weeks, months. They will have trouble engaging anything non-related which can include basic needs, but not always.

Usually, they will still eat, sleep, move, and hydrate as their normal routine dictates. However, they may add a layer of imagination or apply elements from their interest onto those tasks. For example, if their special interest is a story about vampires, they may have more interest in eating red meat, or drinking red drinks, or being nocturnal. Or they may simply constantly have a resource about vampires with them while doing their normal routine. This can be a profoundly creative asset when understood and accommodated.

While attention is mostly influenced by how our brain processes sensory input, even those with only physical disabilities may experience changes in their attention patterns. As someone with chronic pain, they may develop deep internal worlds where they escape to where their attention can be hyperfocused. But more so, we see that when their pain resolves, they have a burst of energy and hyper-attentiveness where they feel like they can accomplish anything.

Someone who has a particular sense that is disabled may have enhanced ability in another sense that they can process in a hyper-attentive way. This can be a tool they use to concentrate on their work. For example, a blind person who has hyper-sensitive hearing may find that manipulating the sound around them allows them to focus on their task or project more deeply.

But these often come like rain storms. They aren't usually predictable, and they don't always last the same amount of time. Instead of punishing ourselves when we can't pay attention, we can honor the process of data collection. Then we can prepare that interest-driven data to be at hand when our concentration becomes focused. This requires the collection system we talked about earlier.

It also means recognizing that different attention patterns serve different phases of creativity. The broad, yet fickle fixations that make us appear distracted may be perfect for initial ideation. The narrow, intense focus might be ideal for revision or completion. Neither is inherently better — they're tools for different creative tasks.

CREATING SUPPORT STRUCTURES TO HELP US GET STARTED

Many neurodivergent and disabled storytellers struggle not with sustaining attention once engaged, but with initiating the creative process. Executive function challenges, pain management, energy limitations, and anxiety can make starting a creative session feel impossible.

Liberation comes from building personalized scaffolding that helps bridge this initiation gap. While timers, schedules, and accountability partners can help all creatives, there are other ways that neurodivergent, chronically ill, and disabled storytellers find useful.

These might include:
- **Body-doubling:** Working alongside someone else, either in person or virtually.
- **Anchoring:** Attaching creative work to existing habits rather than trying to establish new routines.

- **On-ramping:** Creating routines that make starting a gradual process rather than abrupt.
- **Staging:** Setting up your creative environment so that everything you need to have is there and visual reminders help you stick to your process to minimize decision fatigue.

By acknowledging the initiation challenge and creating supports that address it specifically, you stop seeing yourself as "unmotivated" and start recognizing the legitimate barriers you face — and how to work with them rather than against them.

The path to more sustainable attention isn't about focusing more — it's about removing the unnecessary burdens that prevent us from fully engaging with what matters most. When we honor our attention limitations instead of fighting them, we discover we're capable of more than we realized — just not in the ways we've been taught to expect.

DISCOVER YOUR ATTENTION LANDSCAPE EXERCISE

For one week, observe your natural attention patterns without trying to change them. Note when your focus narrows, when it broadens, when it shifts rapidly, and when it settles. Record these observations in whatever format works for you — written notes, voice memos, color-coded charts, or visual maps.

Notice:
- What times of day that different attention states are more likely?
- What environmental factors affect your focus?
- How your attention changes when your physiological condition fluctuates.
- What subjects or activities naturally draw and hold your interest?
- What happens just before you enter states of hyperfocus?

At the end of the week, look for patterns. When is your attention naturally suited for gathering ideas? When is it primed for developing them? When is it ready to refine them?

Create a personal ***Attention Map*** that helps you align creative tasks with your natural cognitive rhythms rather than fighting against them.

Use this map to design a creative practice that works with your brain instead of against it. Build scaffolding that honors the full range of your attention states as valuable parts of the storytelling process.

TRANSFORM SENSORY EXPERIENCE INTO CREATIVE MATERIAL

Choose a comfortable environment where you can

control sensory input to whatever degree you need. Select one sensory channel to explore (sound, vision, touch, smell, taste, or interoceptive/proprioceptive awareness).

For fifteen minutes, allow yourself to experience this sensory channel without trying to direct or narrow your attention. Notice what draws you, what patterns emerge, what memories or associations arise. Record your experience in whatever form feels accessible — words, images, voice notes, movement, or any combination.

Look for story elements in your sensory experience:
- What characters might perceive the world this way?
- What settings contain these sensory qualities?
- What conflicts might arise from different sensory perceptions?
- What metaphors does this sensory experience suggest?

Keep a collection of these sensory explorations as raw material for your stories, recognizing that your unique sensory processing is a creative asset, not a liability.

Practice translating between sensory channels. What would this sound look like? How would this texture sound? Develop the rich, cross-sensory descriptions that make your storytelling distinctive.

Pocket Note: Your attention isn't wrong. It's distinctly yours, and it leads to stories only you can tell. By embracing rather than fighting your natural patterns, you don't just become a more productive storyteller—you become a more authentic one.

CHAPTER 6: Being Kind to Our Creative Selves

"The true nature of the human heart is as whimsical as spring weather. All signals may aim toward a fall of rain when suddenly the skies will clear."
— *Maya Angelou.*

THE MYTH: Our Worth Depends on What We Create

Imagine creativity as a woodland ecosystem. In this landscape, we've been taught to see our storytelling as a tree farm — constantly producing identical rows of trees, measuring their height, and quantifying their quality. Society rewards each story that reaches maturity, packages it up, and sends it out into the world to be consumed.

But we are complex, adaptive, nuanced storytellers creating unique stories. Our worth cannot be reduced to simple metrics.

WHY MEASURING OURSELVES BY OUTPUT HURTS

When we internalize the myth that our value correlates with our productivity, we transform our relationship with creativity from one of co-creation to one of extraction. We begin to see our minds and bodies as resources to be exploited rather than living systems to be nurtured. For neurodivergent, chronically ill, and disabled storytellers, like us, this extractive relationship becomes particularly devastating.

This myth manifests in our daily experience as:
- Crushing guilt when pain or fatigue prevent us from writing.
- Shame that accompanies our executive dysfunction.
- Anxiety that builds when our processing speed misses an arbitrary deadline.
- Self-doubt that emerges during necessary rest periods.

These emotional burdens don't just feel terrible, they actively impede creativity. Preoccupation with measuring our worth by productivity triggers stress responses that make meaningful work even harder. The resulting anxiety narrows our thinking precisely when we need it to expand, generating a cruel cycle where the pressure to produce makes bringing stories into the world increasingly impossible.

For those with chronic health issues, this myth adds another layer of harm. On days we feel well, we overextend, trying to compensate for days we struggle to function. This boom-and-bust cycle reduces both well-being and creative capacity. Measuring our artistic selves by output encourages us to see our natural rhythms as failures rather than information. It defines our limits as weaknesses rather than boundaries to be honored.

Most perniciously, this myth steals our joy. When producing stories becomes primarily a means of proving our worth, we lose access to the intrinsic pleasure, curiosity, and play that fuel authentic expression. We become unable to take risks, experiment, or follow unusual insights — the very elements that make our stories remarkable.

CONVENTIONAL SUCCESS METRICS UNDERVALUE UNSEEN WORK

The traditional markers of creative success are

fundamentally broken. The metrics we're taught to value — like word counts, videos produced, pages completed, submissions sent, or publications secured — capture only what we can see. They fail to account for the vast root system of creative effort that happens beneath the surface.

What others see as hours spent "daydreaming" is actually the essential work of incubating ideas and making unexpected connections. It's when our subconscious minds solve narrative problems. It's when our sensory processing feeds our unique descriptions. It's the energy spent managing physical symptoms while simultaneously trying to create. The emotional labor of accessing, understanding, and translating human experience into stories.

For neurodivergent minds, this invisible work constitutes an even larger proportion of the creative process. Like how an autistic author processes sensory information differently before translating it onto the page. Or the ADHD playwright generates brilliant connections but requires time to structure it into engaging dialogue. Or how a chronically ill content creator must carefully allocate limited energy across both symptom management and artistic visuals. These are vital creative work that conventional metrics render invisible.

Even the terminology we use betrays this limited understanding. We talk about "writer's block" as if it's a failure state rather than potentially a necessary phase of integration. We speak of "discipline" as if consistent daily output matters more than the quality of attention we bring to our work. We celebrate "pushing through" while dismissing the wisdom that comes from resting our bodies and manuscripts.

The cost of these narrow metrics isn't just emotional, it's creative. When we discount the value of contemplation, curation, and percolation, we push ourselves toward familiar patterns and traditional structures. We avoid the messy, cyclical pathways that often lead to our most original work. We sacrifice depth for speed, nuance for productivity, and authenticity for consistency.

REWARDS COME NOT ONLY FROM FINISHING

Our creativity is not a factory assembly line. Some days, progress looks like staring out the window. Other days, it's a single well-crafted sentence. Both are valid. Both are work.

The myth that only completed work has value creates a strange, creative-hostage situation. It tells us that satisfaction, pride, and meaning exist exclusively at the finish line. It completely discounts the journey as nothing but a struggle to be endured. For storytellers whose conditions make working inconsistent, this myth sets up an impossible equation. If only completed projects count, and finishing is particularly challenging, then our creative practice holds no real value.

This fixation on the final product ignores how our brains experience reward and meaning. Neurologically, we're designed to find satisfaction in many aspects of creativity beyond finishing.

The moment of insight when a new idea emerges.
- The pleasure of finding exactly the right word.
- The deep flow that comes from being immersed in creative work.
- The sense of discovery when characters or stories reveal unexpected dimensions.
- The embodied satisfaction of engaging with language, imagery, and narrative.

When we restrict ourselves to finding value only in the final product, we miss these crucial rewards. We become fixated on external validation rather than internal experience. We lose the ability to recognize and celebrate incremental progress. This feast-or-famine approach to creative satisfaction is unsustainable for those of us with inconsistent abilities and capacities.

In truth, we're storytellers even when we're not actively writing — just as a tree remains a tree even when not visibly growing. Our creative identity isn't contingent on constant production. Our worth as storytellers exists in the distinct way we perceive and process the world, whether or not those perceptions make it onto the page.

THE TRUTH: Self-Validation Leads to Better Story

The myth of constant ever-upward momentum permeates our creative culture. In reality, creative development moves in spirals rather than straight lines. We revisit similar territory at deeper levels. We experience breakthroughs followed by integration periods that appear like regression but are actually essential consolidation. We encounter thresholds that require rest before crossing.

These valleys in our creative landscape aren't failures or detours. They're integral parts of the journey. The fallow periods that look stagnant might be when our most important neural rewiring occurs. When our unconscious minds are solving problems that our conscious efforts couldn't resolve.

CRITICAL ROLE OF SELF-COMPASSION

Practicing self-compassion means developing relationships with our creative selves that aren't conditioned around constant productivity. It means speaking to ourselves with the same understanding we would offer a friend navigating similar challenges. We must recognize our fluctuating capacity isn't a character flaw, but an element to be worked within.

This compassionate stance creates psychological safety, which is a prerequisite for authentic, creative expression. When we no longer fear our own judgment for having inconsistent output, we can take the risks necessary for meaningful work. We can explore uncomfortable territory, experiment with approaches that might fail, and access the vulnerability that gives our stories resonance and truth.

Self-compassion helps us recalibrate our expectations to match reality, not just ideals. On days when our conditions flare or our executive function wanes, self-compassion helps us recognize that maintaining creative connection through small acts is a significant achievement. On days when capacity expands, self-compassion helps us channel energy effectively without overextending.

Perhaps most importantly, self-compassion releases us from the shame that blocks creative flow. Shame creates physiological stress responses that impair the neural networks involved in imagination, connection-making, and narrative thinking. By practicing compassion toward our own natural rhythms, we maintain access to our full creative faculties even during challenging periods.

COMPARING OURSELVES TO OTHERS DISTORTS OUR SELF-WORTH

Comparison is the thief of creative joy. Each storyteller's path is uniquely shaped by their body, their experiences, their neural landscape. What looks like slow growth to an outside observer might be a profound, unobservable transformation.

In the age of social media and public productivity trackers, we're bombarded with curated glimpses of other creators' processes and milestones. We see their word counts, publication announcements, and finished projects without witnessing the messy reality behind them. For neurodivergent, chronically ill, and disabled storytellers, these comparisons become a toxic reminder of the gap between conventional productivity and our complex creative realities.

This comparison game obscures the radically different conditions under which we each create. Equating our outputs to others is like equating the speed of vehicles with different engines, driving on different terrains, and carrying different loads.

It also falsely suggests there's a single valid formula to creative development.

Standardization erases the distinctiveness that makes our work valuable. Our desire to meet or exceed external metrics rather than internal alignment encourages us to prioritize conformity over curiosity, validation over exploration, and recognizable success over meaningful risk.

Most insidiously, comparison transplants others' definitions of success into our creative practice without examining whether they serve our actual goals. These borrowed values create constant inner conflict, splitting our attention between what others appear to accomplish and what our systems actually need.

FREEING OURSELVES FROM THE COMPARISON GAME

Breaking free from comparison requires recognizing its distorted nature. We cannot compare our complete reality, including our struggles, setbacks, and invisible work with others' curated presentations of their process. It's an inherently imbalanced equation that will always generate feelings of inadequacy, regardless of actual creative development.

It also requires developing resilience strategies for managing the inevitable moments when comparison arises.

These might include:
- Remembering that we only see glimpses of other creators' lives to help maintain perspective.
- Cultivating relationships with fellow storytellers who share similar challenges.
- Documenting our own progress in ways that make our growth visible to ourselves.
- Deliberately seeking out role models with similar conditions who create in non-conventional methods.

- Practicing gentle redirection when comparison thoughts arise.

Perhaps most importantly, breaking free from comparison means recognizing that your value as a creator never depended on how your process or output compares to others'. The legitimacy of your creative identity stands independent of external markers. Your worth as a storyteller exists not in relation to others' achievements but in your distinctive way of perceiving, processing, and expressing human experience — a perspective the world needs precisely because no one else can offer it.

***Journal Reflection:** Instead of asking, "Am I keeping up with other creators?" We can ask, "Is this approach serving my specific creative needs? Does this practice honor my body's actual capabilities? Am I making the kind of work that matters to me, in a way that's sustainable for my particular system?"*

THE HIDDEN VALUE IN UNFINISHED PROJECTS

No seed becomes a towering tree in a single season. Some germinate slowly. Some rest underground, gathering strength. Our creative projects are similar. An "unfinished" project is not a failure — it's research. It's learning. It's preparation.

Incomplete works often carry the stigma of failure. We're taught to view abandoned drafts, paused projects, and ideas that never fully materialize as evidence of inadequate commitment or skill. This perspective contradicts the path diverse brains and bodies take from story conception to completion. Our paths frequently include pauses, shifts in direction, and extended incubation periods.

Immense value lays hidden in what appears to be "unfinished" work. Every project we begin contributes to our growth as storytellers in ways that often remain invisible until much later. Each time we play with story, we develop our skills and flex our creative muscles.

The dialogue exercises in an abandoned screenplay might inform the natural conversation in a future short story. The world-building for a paused fantasy novel might provide the detailed setting for a completed flash fiction piece years later.

Unfinished projects often stall because we've encountered creative problems that we don't yet have the skills to solve. Recognizing these issues — even without resolution — is crucial developmental work.

The mystery novel we set aside because we couldn't make the clues coherent teaches us about narrative causality. The memoir that stalled because the emotional material was too raw shows us where we need healing before artistic transformation will become possible.

Ideas, images, characters, and themes from unfinished work don't disappear. They decompose into rich creative material that nourishes future projects. Sometimes, the secondary character that didn't work for one project may become the perfect point of view for a new series. Or a thematic question we couldn't answer in an abandoned essay resurfaces years later when life experience provides new insight.

Each unfinished project teaches us something about our creative process. The novel draft abandoned after trying to write at night reveals we're a morning creator. The story collection that stalled when we tried to outline each piece shows us that we thrive on discovery-based methods. These insights about process are invaluable even when the projects that generated them remain incomplete.

By honoring the hidden value of unfinished work, we reclaim the full spectrum of our creative journey. We transform what feels like a history of false starts and stalled efforts into a rich, complex development process uniquely suited to our lived experience. One that generates exactly the creative voice only we can offer.

Journal Reflection: *What unfinished project have you given yourself the most grief for not completing? What skill/technique did you learn while creating it? Looking back, what stalled your progress? What permission do you* *need to give yourself to either let this project go or to pick this project back up?*

OUR LIBERATION: Compassionate Creative Journaling

HEALING STORIES TO REPLACE LIMITING BELIEFS

The stories we tell ourselves about our creative process shape our experience as powerfully as any external circumstance. For storytellers like us, these internal narratives often contain harmful myths absorbed from a culture that privileges neurotypical, able-bodied ways of creating. Liberation begins when we consciously craft new stories to replace these limiting beliefs.

Consider the common internal narrative, "If I were a real storyteller, I would work every day." This story ignores the reality of chronic conditions, energy limitations, and processing differences. A healing counter-narrative might be, "My inconsistent writing schedule reflects my body's changing needs, not my commitment to storytelling."

Or the limiting belief, "My creative worth depends on finishing projects and sharing them with the world." This narrative harms those of us for whom completing their work requires navigating additional barriers. A compassionate alternative would be, "The value of my creative practice exists in my relationship with my imagination, not just in finished work. My explorations have inherent worth, whether or not they result in publication."

Compassionate journaling creates space to identify these limiting stories and develop healing alternatives. Through regular reflection, we can:

- Notice when internal criticism follows patterns of ableist or neurotypical expectations.
- Question whether these expectations actually serve our unique creative process.
- Craft alternative narratives that honor our bodies, minds, and authentic creative rhythms.
- Repeatedly reinforce these healing stories until they become our default self-talk.

This practice isn't about positive thinking or denial of real challenges. Instead, it's about rewriting the stories we tell ourselves to accurately reflect the complex reality of creating while neurodivergent, chronically ill, or disabled.

When we journal about our creative experience with compassion rather than judgment, we transform our relationship with creativity itself. Our connection with our creativity changes from demanding and punitive to collaborative and respectful. This shift not only feels better. It creates the psychological safety necessary for authentic expression and sustainable story crafting.

CREATING OUR OWN DEFINITION OF SUCCESS

The standardized markers of creative success, like publication, audience size, professional recognition, and consistent productivity, were not designed for storytellers like us. Liberation comes from crafting alternative definitions that honor our actual experiences, values, and capabilities.

Compassionate journaling offers a structured space to explore what meaningful success looks like for our specific creative reality.

Through reflective writing, we can:

- Identify which conventional success markers trigger shame or inadequacy.
- Explore which aspects of creativity bring genuine satisfaction.
- Consider what sustainability looks like for our particular mind and body.
- Articulate values that matter more to us than conventional achievements.
- Craft definitions of success that remain achievable despite fluctuations in our symptoms or capacity.

This isn't about lowering standards. It's about creating appropriate ones. For example, a chronically ill author might define success as maintaining creative connection during flare-ups, rather than writing through pain. An autistic storyteller might value capturing sensory experience with precision over appealing to mainstream audiences. A creator with ADHD might prioritize completing projects that sustain interest, rather than working methodically on a single project.

Your personalized definition might include elements like:

- Moments of genuine creative joy or flow, regardless of output.
- Connections between unrelated ideas that only your mind would make.
- Accurately representing experiences rarely seen in mainstream stories.
- Creating in ways that honor rather than harm your body's needs.
- Maintaining creative identity through varying levels of capacity.
- Finding language for experiences previously unnamed.

Through regular journaling about what constitutes meaningful creative success for you, these personalized definitions gradually replace internalized conventional standards. You'll start judging your creative work by your own standards, not others', leading to genuine satisfaction.

RECLAIMING OUR VOICE FROM HARMFUL EXPECTATIONS

Our most powerful stories emerge when we write from our authentic experience rather than contorting ourselves to meet external expectations. Compassionate journaling creates a private, judgment-free space to rediscover and strengthen our natural voice, unlimited by marketplace expectations or neurotypical preferences.

Through regular reflection, we can begin to notice when we're censoring our natural way of seeing and expressing. Keeping a record of the unique patterns, preoccupations, and perspectives that create our authentic voice, we can slowly unearth the distinct features of it.

We can also identify external rules we've internalized about what stories "should" look like. Then we can go deeper and explore what emerges when we temporarily suspend these rules. One fun way is to ask "what if…" and see where that possibility leads. If you can't imagine it in your real life, put yourself into a fictional world.

When we practice trusting our natural storytelling instincts, even when they diverge from convention, we build our skills and confidence. This reclamation might involve embracing elements that traditional advice discourages but reflects neurodivergent or disabled experiences. This might look like non-linear narrative structures that mirror how our mind processes information. Or as sensory-rich description that captures our distinct perception.

As we explore our own lives, our pacing may reflect our unique relationships with time and energy. Or we might create characters whose motivations and behaviors reflect neurodivergent or disabled realities like our own. Themes will naturally emerge from our lived experience rather than tropes.

Journaling about these elements helps us recognize that what might be labeled as craft "weaknesses" from a mainstream perspective are often the very aspects that make our voice distinctive and valuable. When we document the moments where our natural expression feels most alive, we build trust in our unique creative instincts.

The literary world needs stories about neurodivergent, chronically ill, and disabled experiences. But it also needs stories told through our perspectives, with all the structural and stylistic differences that entails.

LEARNING FROM PROJECTS WE DIDN'T FINISH

Unfinished projects hold valuable insights about our creative process, preferences, and growth—but only if we approach them with curiosity rather than shame. Compassionate journaling transforms abandoned drafts from evidence of failure into rich sources of self-knowledge.

Instead of filing away unfinished work with a sense of

defeat, we can use reflective writing to:
- Identify patterns across projects that didn't reach completion.
- Explore what initially sparked enthusiasm and when/why it waned.
- Consider whether the project stalled for internal reasons like skill gaps, loss of interest. Or external ones such as flares, life circumstances.
- Recognize what the project taught us, even in its incomplete state.
- Honor the legitimate reasons for setting it aside rather than forcing continuation.

This reflective practice can reveal important insights about your creative process. Perhaps you consistently lose momentum during the same phase of projects, suggesting a specific skill area to develop. Or maybe certain project types require more energy than is sustainable for your current capacity.

You might discover that your interest revolves in cycles that could be anticipated and accommodated. Perhaps your authentic voice was being suppressed by trying to write in styles that don't align with your natural expression. You might identify specific supports or structures that were missing when projects stalled.

By journaling about unfinished work with compassion rather than criticism, you transform what feels like a history of failure into valuable research about your creative needs. These insights become the foundation for designing future projects and systems that better align with your capabilities and interests. This will increase the likelihood of completion and satisfaction.

This approach also allows you to consciously "compost" elements from unfinished projects — identifying characters, settings, themes, or ideas worth preserving for future work. Through reflective writing, you can document these valuable elements, ensuring they remain accessible even as you release shame associated with the original unfinished project.

CREATING YOUR COMPASSIONATE CREATIVE JOURNAL

Find a journal that feels inviting and accessible for your lowest energy days. That might be physical or digital, depending on your needs. If physical, consider spiral bound versus spine bound and which you work better with.

Keep whatever you need, like pens, stickers, a charger, or stylus with this journal in the space where you intend to reflect. Make the spot cozy and comfortable.

Establish a sustainable rhythm. Rather than committing to daily journaling, which can become another source of pressure, consider what frequency works best for your fluctuating capacity. Maybe it's three times a week. Maybe it's on days when pain or anxiety are below a certain threshold. Maybe it's while waiting for medical appointments.

Create entry points for different capacity levels. Develop a menu of journaling approaches for different energy, focus, and pain levels:

- **High-capacity days:** Extended reflection on creative patterns, detailed exploration of project challenges.
- **Medium-capacity days:** Structured responses to specific prompts, brief scene explorations.
- **Low-capacity days:** Single-word responses, voice recordings instead of writing, simple check-ins with creative self.

Track your patterns without judgment. Include simple notation about your physical and mental state alongside entries. You can keep track of energy level, pain level, focus quality, etc. This isn't to berate yourself for low-capacity days, but to recognize patterns in your creative rhythm.

Balance reflection with creation. Use the journal both to process your creative experience and to engage in small creative acts. This prevents the journal from becoming focused on limitations.

Periodically review past entries with curiosity rather than criticism. Look for patterns in what supports or hinders your creativity. Highlight evidence of growth or insights that weren't obvious in the moment. Then note any recurring themes or preoccupations that might inform future projects. If you notice unhelpful narratives, give them a special mark that you can easily find, so you can consciously reframe them at a future session.

Designate a section of your journal to document insights about your unique creative process as they emerge. You might use the last ten pages or use a special highlighter color to note those revelations. This becomes a personalized creative guide you can reference during challenging periods.

Remember, the purpose of compassionate, creative journaling isn't to create another obligation or measurement tool. It's establishing a consistent, gentle dialogue with your creative self that honors the complex reality of constructing stories while neurodivergent, chronically ill, or disabled. This ongoing conversation becomes the foundation for a sustainable creative practice built around your actual needs and strengths.

Through this practice, your journal becomes not just a record of your creative journey, but an active participant in it. Your journal is a private space where limiting beliefs can be questioned, authentic voice is strengthened, and your unique creative identity is continuously affirmed, regardless of external outcomes.

PRACTICE: JOURNAL IDEAS FOR WHEN PROGRESS FEELS INVISIBLE

On days when our conditions flare, executive function wanes, or creative momentum seems lost, structured journaling prompts help us maintain connection to our creativity while acknowledging current limitations. These prompts create touchpoints for your creative identity, even when progress isn't possible.

Sensory Awareness Prompts
- What's one sound in your environment right now that other people might not notice?
- Describe the quality of the light in your current space using an unexpected comparison.
- What's the most interesting texture within reach? How might it feel different for one of your characters?
- If your current emotional state had a taste, what would it be?

Creative Identity Prompts
- What's one way your divergent brain or disabled body enhances your storytelling?
- Describe a moment when your creativity surprised you in its resilience.
- What creative strength do you have that you don't give yourself enough credit for?
- How has your relationship with creativity evolved since you began understanding your condition?

Process Reflection Prompts

- When do you feel most connected to your creative self? What elements are present in those moments?
- What's one small adjustment that might make creating more accessible during difficult seasons?
- What does your mind/body need today that will support your long-term creative development?
- How might today's limitations be informing your understanding of experiences you might write about?

Project Connection Prompts
- Write one line of dialogue for a character you're developing, without worrying about context.
- What's one question you're currently curious about related to your project?
- If you could add one unexpected element to your current story, what would it be?
- Write a six-word story set in the world of your current project.

Creative Permission Prompts
- What would you create if no one would ever read it?
- What would your ten-year-old self want you to write about?
- If your creative voice could speak directly to you, what would it say today?
- What story feels too personal, too complex, or too unconventional to tell? Why?

Pocket Note: *Our liberation lies in recognizing that even on days when conventional progress seems impossible, we can still engage with our creativity in ways that honor our current capacity.*

CHAPTER 7: Creating Story in Community

"Spring adds new life and new beauty to all that is."
— *Jessica Harrison*

THE MYTH: Real Artists Work Alone

The image of the solitary genius is a dangerous fiction. This narrative serves neither creativity nor humanity. It's a myth crafted to isolate us, to convince each storyteller that their struggles are personal failures rather than systemic barriers.

THE HARMFUL IDEA OF THE CREATIVE HERMIT

History reveals that creative breakthroughs emerge not from isolation but from rich networks of exchange. Even famously solitary figures like Emily Dickinson maintained an extensive correspondence that influenced their work. The Renaissance flourished through artistic communities, not lone visionaries. The most innovative scientific discoveries come from collaborative teams, not isolated thinkers.

Yet we cling to this romantic fantasy of the creative hermit because it supports other harmful narratives — that suffering is necessary for art, that "real artists" must sacrifice relationships, that meaningful work happens only in dramatic isolation. These beliefs damage creators, leading to unnecessary loneliness, burnout, and despair.

The myth also conveniently obscures structural inequalities. When we celebrate only the individual's "genius," we ignore how privilege, access, and support systems enable creative work. Not everyone can afford "a room of one's own" or freedom from financial pressures.

A healthier vision recognizes creativity as inherently communal. Ideas need nurturing through conversation, feedback, and shared inspiration. Creativity thrives when we acknowledge our interdependence rather than posturing as self-sufficient islands.

By dismantling the myth of the creative hermit, we can build more sustainable, accessible, and honest creative practices. We can create supportive communities that distribute both the joys and burdens of making meaningful work, recognizing that no voice emerges in a vacuum.

HOW FOCUSING ONLY ON INDIVIDUAL CREATIVITY HURTS US

This myth of the lone creator is particularly brutal for neurodivergent, disabled, and chronically ill storytellers, like us. It erases the intricate web of support, adaptation, and collective wisdom that has always been the true engine of creative work. Our stories have never been solo journeys. They are tapestries woven with threads of shared experience, mutual aid, and radical interdependence.

When we glorify the solitary artist working tirelessly through the night, we create impossible standards that exclude those whose bodies and minds work differently. The neurodivergent creator who needs specific environmental conditions, the disabled author who relies on assistive technology, the chronically ill artist who works in sporadic bursts between periods of rest — all are deemed "less dedicated" under this harmful paradigm.

History tells a different truth. Frida Kahlo painted from her bed. Helen Keller's work was made possible through collaboration with Anne Sullivan. Stephen Hawking's revolutionary theories emerged with technological and human assistance. Interdependence did not diminish their brilliance, it enabled it.

The individualist myth also conveniently absolves society of its responsibility to create accessible conditions for all creators. By framing creative success as purely personal determination, we ignore how systematic barriers exclude diverse voices from cultural conversations.

Embracing collective creativity isn't just about fairness. It enriches our cultural landscape. When we acknowledge creativity as inherently collaborative, we open doors to varied perspectives and innovative approaches. We recognize that caregivers, assistants, editors, and friends are not peripheral to creative work, but integral to it.

True creative liberation comes when we honor the intricate networks that nurture each story.

THE ERASURE OF SHARED WISDOM

No story emerges in a vacuum. Every word is shaped by listening, by conversing, and by the subtle energetic exchanges that happen when humans connect. Our creativity is not a solitary act, but a collaborative symphony.

When we examine the origins of any creative work, we find countless invisible contributors. The grandmother's tale that sparked a novelist's imagination. The teacher who introduced a specific technique. The friend whose casual comment unlocked a new perspective. The countless predecessors whose innovations form the foundation upon which new work stands. These influences are rarely acknowledged in our celebration of individual genius.

Indigenous knowledge systems have long recognized this truth. Many Native cultures understand creativity as communal property, with stories belonging not to individuals but to communities. Art emerges from collective experience and returns to serve collective needs. This wisdom stands in stark contrast to Western notions of intellectual property and individual ownership.

The erasure of shared wisdom particularly disadvantages marginalized creators. When dominant cultures appropriate techniques, themes, and aesthetic innovations from underrepresented groups without acknowledgment, they perpetuate a harmful fiction that creativity springs solely from privileged individuals rather than from diverse communities.

Even our language betrays this bias. We award prizes to individuals rather than communities. We ask artists about their influences as an afterthought, not as the central story of how their work came to be.

By reclaiming the collaborative nature of creativity, we honor truth and foster generative creative practices. We shift from competitive isolation to networks of mutual support, where ideas flow freely, nurtured by many hands, hearts, and minds working in concert.

THE TRUTH: Creativity Thrives in Connection

CREATIVITY AS A SHARED PROCESS

Creativity has never truly been the domain of isolated geniuses, despite what our cultural mythology suggests. When we examine the historical record, we discover that even our most celebrated creators were deeply embedded in networks of influence, support, and exchange.

Einstein corresponded with numerous physicists while developing relativity. Virginia Woolf's literary innovations emerged within the stimulating conversations of the Bloomsbury Group. Jazz greats developed their revolutionary styles through late-night jam sessions and mutual inspiration.

The creative process itself demands connection. Ideas need testing, refinement, and the friction of outside perspective to reach their potential. A thought kept entirely to oneself rarely evolves beyond its initial spark. When shared, even if only with a trusted friend or mentor, it begins to breathe and grow in new ways, revealing its deeper possibilities.

This shared nature of creativity extends beyond direct

collaboration. Every creator draws from a vast cultural inheritance — techniques, knowledge, and aesthetic traditions. We build upon existing foundations even when working in apparent solitude. The poet writing alone at dawn is still engaged in dialogue with every poem they've ever read, every conversation about language they've ever had.

THE FREEING POWER OF SUPPORTIVE CREATIVE NETWORKS

When we embrace creativity as inherently connected, something remarkable happens. We become free. The crushing weight of sole responsibility lifts. We no longer need to be the exclusive source of brilliance, originality, and perfect execution. We can acknowledge our limitations without shame, knowing that where our abilities end, another's begin.

Supportive creative networks distribute both the burdens and joys of creative work. In a healthy collaborative environment, rest becomes possible. One person can step back when energy wanes, trusting others to carry the project forward. Ideas find multiple pathways to expression rather than depending on a single individual's capacity to bring them to life.

These networks also create safety for risk-taking. When we know others will catch us if we fall, we dare more boldly.

Experimentation flourishes in environments where failure is met not with judgment but with curiosity and collective problem-solving. Innovation emerges not from isolated brilliance but from communities where wild ideas are welcomed, refined through dialogue, and collectively brought to fruition.

REIMAGINING COMMUNITY IN WAYS THAT WORK FOR US

Embracing creativity as connection doesn't mean forcing everyone into the same collaborative model. Instead, it invites us to reimagine community in ways that honor diverse needs and working styles. The introverted storyteller might find their ideal connection in an online feedback group with clear boundaries. The intermittently available creator with chronic illness might thrive in an asynchronous collaboration where contribution timelines remain flexible.

Digital spaces have expanded our possibilities for creative connection while challenging us to design more intentional communities. We can create networks that span geographic boundaries while maintaining intimate spaces for vulnerable exchange. We can develop collaborative practices that honor neurodiversity, disability, and varying energy levels rather than defaulting to models that work only for the most privileged bodies and minds.

The key lies in acknowledging interdependence as our natural state, rather than viewing it as weakness. When we stop trying to perform as self-sufficient creative genius, we can openly negotiate our genuine needs and boundaries. We can articulate what we bring to collaborative spaces and what support we require. We can create mutual aid structures that ensure no creator struggles alone against systemic barriers.

By reimagining community in ways that work for diverse creators, we don't just make creative practice more sustainable for individuals, we enrich our collective cultural landscape. Stories emerge from perspectives previously silenced. Methods evolve to accommodate different ways of knowing and creating. The resulting work carries the richness of multiple voices, experiences, and ways of seeing the world.

***Journal Reflection:** Creativity thrives in connection. Who helps you engage in the beautiful, challenging work of bringing new things into being?*

OUR LIBERATION: Building Supportive Creative Networks

Connection is not a luxury. It is a fundamental creative resource.

True creative community recognizes that:

- Access needs are not inconveniences — they are fundamental human rights.
- Communication has countless languages.
- Rest is productive.
- Showing up looks different for everyone.
- Creativity flows through relationship.

REIMAGINING COMMUNITY

Supportive creative networks are ecosystems, not hierarchies. They are living organisms that adapt, that breathe, that make space for everyone's unique brilliance. When we envision creative communities as complex, interconnected systems rather than rigid structures, we open possibilities for more genuine and generative collaboration.

Consent-based participation forms the foundation of healthy creative ecosystems. Each member actively chooses their level of involvement, with clear protocols for proposing, accepting, and declining collaborative opportunities. This stands in stark contrast to traditional models where participation is often coerced through economic necessity or professional pressure. When consent drives engagement, both the work and the relationships surrounding it flourish.

Flexible engagement models recognize that creative energy ebbs and flows. Some contribute intensely for short periods, others steadily over time. Sustainable communities accommodate different rhythms — the early morning creator, the weekend warrior, the sporadic but brilliant contributor. They build structures where consistent presence isn't conflated with commitment or value.

Trauma-informed communication acknowledges that many creators carry wounds from previous collaborative experiences. These communities develop practices that minimize harm, like clear boundaries, transparent decision-making processes, and methods for addressing conflict that don't replicate power imbalances. They create safety not through avoiding tough conversations, but through approaching them with care.

Multiple entry and exit points ensure communities remain permeable rather than closed. Newcomers can join without climbing impossible barriers to entry. Members can step back when needed without burning bridges. This permeability keeps creative ecosystems vibrant, preventing stagnation while maintaining enough continuity for trust to develop.

Celebrating diverse contributions means recognizing that creativity manifests beyond the final product. The person who asks the clarifying question, who maintains the shared calendar, who checks in on a struggling member are essential to the ecosystem's health. By valuing different forms of creative participation, these communities access broader pools of wisdom and avoid reproducing harmful patterns of recognition.

When implemented thoughtfully, these principles transform creative practice from a solitary struggle to a communal journey — one where individual brilliance is not suppressed but amplified through meaningful connection.

STRATEGIES FOR THRIVING TOGETHER

Creative communities thrive when they intentionally design structures that support diverse needs and working styles. These practical strategies transform abstract principles into tangible practices that foster both individual wellbeing and collective flourishing.

When creating a community:

- Offer multiple communication channels that accommodate different strengths and challenges. Some members may articulate ideas most clearly in writing, others through conversation. Some may need visual aids to process information effectively. By providing text-based, verbal, and visual options for engagement, communities ensure no one's contributions are lost due to communication format.
- Create clear opt-in/opt-out processes for discussions and projects. Explicit consent mechanisms allow members to manage their energy

and attention without guilt. This might look like color-coded energy signaling systems in meetings, transparent project commitment documentation, or regular check-ins about capacity.

- Respect different processing speeds by building pause points into collaborative work. Quick thinkers and those who need more reflection time both have valuable perspectives. Communities should build in "marination periods" before decisions and normalize phrases like "I need to think about this and circle back" to access deeper collective wisdom.

- Use collaborative tools that allow asynchronous participation so geography, time zones, energy levels, and life circumstances don't exclude potential contributors. Shared documents with comment features, project management platforms with clear task ownership, and recording options for synchronous meetings extend participation beyond those who can be present and attentive at specific moments.

- Celebrate each other's access needs as opportunities for innovation rather than burdens. When someone shares what they need to participate fully — whether that's screen reader compatibility, content warnings, or scheduled

breaks — the community gains insights that often improve systems for everyone.
- Create rotating support roles to distribute the care work that sustains creative communities. Designating facilitators, note-takers, time-keepers, and emotional check-in volunteers. Regularly shifting these responsibilities to prevent burnout and build collective skill.
- Practice accountability without punishment by developing response protocols for when harm occurs. Restorative approaches focus on repair and growth rather than shame and exclusion. This creates space for the inevitable mistakes that happen in human connection without destroying trust or relationships.
- Recognize invisible labor through formal acknowledgment systems. The behind-the-scenes work of coordination, emotional support, and maintenance often falls disproportionately on marginalized group members. Communities that track, compensate, and celebrate this essential labor create more sustainable participation patterns.

By implementing these concrete strategies, creative communities move beyond aspirational rhetoric into practical solidarity, creating spaces where diverse creators can truly thrive together.

Pocket Note: *We are not meant to create alone. Our stories gain power through connection, through listening, through seeing each other. Every shared moment is an act of creative liberation.*

PRACTICE: THE COMPASSIONATE COLLABORATION CHART

INTENTION:

To honor the intricate web of support that makes your storytelling possible, to release the shame of interdependence, and to envision new possibilities for creative connection that honor your unique body and mind.

PREPARATION:

Create a safe container. Choose a time when you have energy to spare. Set up any accommodations you need — comfortable seating, voice recording instead of writing, assistive technology, or a trusted scribe.

Gather materials that bring you joy.

- Write one line of dialogue for a character you're developing, without worrying about context.
- Large paper or digital canvas (whatever feels accessible to you)
- Colors that speak to your senses (markers, digital colors, collage materials)

- Comfort items (favorite blanket, tea, fidget objects)
- Optional: gentle music that supports your focus.

THE PRACTICE:

1. *Center yourself with compassion.* Begin by placing yourself at the center of your page — not as an isolated individual, but as a nexus of connection. Draw or write your name with kindness. Take a moment to acknowledge your unique creative gifts and the wisdom your specific embodied experience brings to your storytelling.

2. *Chart your constellation of support.* Radiating outward from yourself, begin charting every form of help that makes your creative work possible. Include:
   - Creative collaborators (blue): Editors, writing group members, mentors, readers who provide feedback
   - Access providers (green): Caregivers, assistive technology, medication, therapies, accessibility tools
   - Emotional anchors (red): Friends who witness your struggles, family who believe in your work, communities that affirm your experience
   - Practical supporters (purple): Those who help with daily needs, transportation, financial support, technical assistance
   - Inspirational sources (yellow): Other disabled artists, ancestral wisdom, spiritual practices, natural environments

For each connection, note not just their presence, but how they specifically make your creative work possible.

3. *Honor the empty spaces with curiosity.* Notice areas where support feels thin or absent. Instead of viewing these as failures, approach them with gentle curiosity.

Ask yourself:
- What forms of support would nourish my creative practice?
- What might be available that I haven't recognized or requested?
- What systems or communities could I help create to fill these gaps?

4. *Envision reciprocity.* For each connection on your chart, consider what you offer in return — not from obligation, but from the natural flow of mutual aid. How does your presence, your story, your perspective enrich those who support you?

5. *Declare your creative birthright.* At the bottom of your chart, complete this sentence with bold, unapologetic strokes:

"My interdependence is not weakness but wisdom. My storytelling matters because…"

INTEGRATION:

Keep your **Compassionate Collaboration Chart** visible in your creative space. Return to it when shame about needing support arises. Update it as your network evolves. Share it with trusted members of your community to make visible the often invisible infrastructure of creative work.

Every successful story throughout history emerged

through collaboration. Your need for support is not the exception, it's the rule. It's the way creativity has always worked. By charting and honoring your creative ecosystem, you are not only liberating yourself but modeling a more honest and sustainable approach to creativity for everyone.

CHAPTER 8: Growing Stories in Spring

"It's spring fever. That is what the name of it is. And when you've got it, you want—oh, you don't quite know what it is you do want, but it just fairly makes your heart ache, you want it so!" — Mark Twain

THE MYTH: Go Big or Go Home

THE LIE THAT ONLY LARGE

PROJECTS MATTER

Spring is the season of renewal and growth. Gardeners plan what they want to plant, and buy seeds and seedlings to fill the space. "Go big or go home," is the season's mantra. Fellow storytellers challenge us to dream big. We're dared to write an epic novel, a screenplay for a feature film, or a Broadway worthy three-act play.

But for many neurodivergent, chronically ill, and disabled storytellers, the joy of planning vies with the pressure to complete it all. The number of steps to finish the project quickly dampens our enthusiasm. Overwhelm then leads to abandoning our plans to do any planting in our creative garden at all.

This harmful cycle ignores the profound impact of smaller creative acts. A well-crafted haiku can alter a reader's perception in seventeen syllables. A thoughtful journal entry might preserve an insight that changes the course of your life years later. A short story shared within a community can create ripples of connection that a novel gathering dust in a drawer cannot.

For bodies and minds that experience fluctuating energy, unpredictable symptoms, or processing differences, smaller creative projects aren't a compromise — they're often the most authentic expression of our lived experience. They honor the episodic nature of our lives, the precious moments of clarity amid brain fog, the bursts of energy between periods of rest.

History offers countless examples of "small" works that transformed culture like Emily Dickinson's compact poems or Franz Kafka's brief parables. These weren't lesser efforts by creators who couldn't manage big projects. They were perfectly sized vessels for the truths they needed to express.

By reclaiming the value of small creative works, we resist the capitalist demand for immediate greatness. We embrace a more sustainable, honest relationship with our creative practice — one that celebrates presence over production, meaning over magnitude.

TYPICAL PROJECT ADVICE IGNORES RESOURCE LIMITS

Many traditional productivity tips do not account for fluctuating energy levels, sensory sensitivities, and the unpredictability of neurodivergence or chronic illness. They rely on linear planning, rigid schedules, and the belief that "consistency is king." But when our bodies and brains refuse to comply with these standards, we feel like we're failing. In reality, the advice is failing us.

Most project management frameworks were designed for neurotypical brains and non-disabled bodies working in predictable environments. The popular instruction to go out into our creative gardens at dawn, pull the weeds of distraction, then dive into planting another row of flowery words assumes we have a reliable energy pattern.

"Push through resistance" ignores that, for many of us, resistance is a crucial bodily signal, not mere procrastination. "Break large projects into equal chunks" fails to recognize that some days offer abundant capacity while others barely permit basic functioning.

These approaches create additional burdens for those with divergent brains and disabled bodies. Beyond the work itself, we must manage the emotional labor of reconciling our lived reality with impossible standards, often internalizing shame when the gap proves unbridgeable. Each deviation from the prescribed plan becomes evidence of personal failure rather than proof of an ill-fitting system.

A more liberating approach recognizes resource fluctuation as reality, not an exception. It honors the wisdom of bodies and brains that demand different rhythms. It celebrates the innovative adaptations that emerge when we work with our unique mental and physical landscapes rather than against them. True productivity comes not from forcing ourselves into standardized methods but from crafting personalized practices that respect our actual resources.

THE HARM OF THE LABELS "SERIOUS" & "HOBBY"

In the literary landscape, the labels "serious storyteller"

and "hobby storyteller" fall like late frost on tender shoots. They arbitrarily determine which creative talents will be nurtured and which will wither under neglect. This false binary damages storytellers like us, whose creative practices don't follow conventional patterns.

Consider the spring garden, where some plants burst dramatically skyward while others spread in quiet networks beneath the soil. Both are vital to the ecosystem, yet our culture celebrates only the visible, consistent growth. The crocus that pushes through snow on its own timeline is no less serious about blooming than the predictable daffodil.

The "serious storyteller" label typically demands daily ambition and consistent results. These requirements ignore our fluctuating energy, processing differences, and access barriers. When disability requires us to write in sporadic bursts, or when chronic pain limits us to dictation rather than typing, or when sensory sensitivities mean we create best in environments deemed "unprofessional," our commitment is questioned rather than our environment adapted. And our need to justify our existence and needs uses up our precious spoons, often faster than trying to earn the "professional" label.

When we get shuffled off into the category of "hobby", we find our stories stifled from growing beyond what we are capable of producing on our own. Few expert gardeners are willing to mentor us. And yet there is freedom given that allows us to experiment freely and to work in community to learn how to nurture different types of stories.

But there is another path. We can learn to value our creative work differently. Like wildflowers reclaiming disturbed ground, we can spread the radical notion that seriousness lies not in conformity to external expectations but in the authentic relationship between creator and creation.

The disabled caregiver writing between medical appointments, the autistic poet crafting one perfect line during a moment of clarity, the author with ADHD who completes projects in hyperfocused bursts are all as serious as the daily novelist. The true dividing line isn't between hobby and professional, but between writing that matters deeply to its creator and writing that doesn't. Everything else is just garden variety prejudice masquerading as merit.

THE TRUTH: Matching Our Projects to Our Resources

DIFFERENT PROJECTS FOR DIFFERENT ENERGY LEVELS

The beauty of storytelling is that it can exist in countless forms, each valid and worthy. Different seasons of life call for different approaches. When energy is abundant, we might dream up ambitious narratives.

When it's scarce, we can nurture smaller creations that still offer profound satisfaction.

For storytellers like us, energy ebbs and flows like spring streams after rainfall. Sometimes it rushes with possibility. Other times it slows to a trickle. Rather than fighting this natural rhythm, we can attune our creative practice to it, selecting projects that match our current capacity.

High-energy days may welcome world-building, research deep-dives, or first drafts where words flow unfiltered. These are the days when the sap runs quick in the trees, when ideas burst forth like new leaves unfurling. We can embrace these moments without expecting them to last indefinitely.

On medium-energy days, drafting or revision work may be more compatible. Like a gardener staking young plants or pruning branches, we may find we make steady progress working scene by scene. A paragraph polished, a character deepened, a plot hole mended — these accomplishments matter.

Low-energy periods call for gentle creative acts. These are useful days to collect sensory details in our creative notebooks, dictate a single vivid memory, or simply listen to the stories others tell. Even rest itself becomes part of the creative cycle. This becomes the fallow time when story seeds germinate and the thematic roots deepen.

By building a diverse project portfolio across various types of work, we create a sustainable creative practice that weathers changing conditions. We learn to recognize which projects nourish us during particular states and to move fluidly between them without judgment.

This approach doesn't diminish our seriousness as storytellers. It demonstrates our sophisticated understanding that creativity, like nature itself, operates in cycles of action and rest. The oak that flexes with the wind stands longer than the one that refuses to bend.

NON-LINEAR APPROACHES FOR DIVERSE MINDS & BODIES

For neurodivergent storytellers, nonlinear thinking is often a strength. Our minds may jump from idea to idea, weaving connections others might miss. Chronically ill creators might move through cycles of productivity and rest, finding insights in both states. By embracing these natural rhythms, we can craft projects that honor our lived experiences.

Traditional creative methodologies focused on rigid outlines, sequential steps, and steady progression may feel foreign to diverse minds. Like forcing a meandering creek into a straight concrete channel, these approaches can dampen the very qualities that make our stories unique.

Consider how an autistic storyteller perceives patterns

and details that may spark unexpected narrative connections, or how someone with ADHD can generate brilliant innovative concepts through associative thinking. These cognitive differences aren't deficits to overcome, but powerful creative assets. The leaps that appear "off-topic" to others often form the basis of our most original insights.

For those with chronic illness or pain, creativity rarely follows a predictable timeline. A flare might interrupt a project mid-sentence, yet the processing that happens during forced rest can yield a deeper understanding of character motivations or thematic elements. The pause becomes part of the process. A necessary winter that makes spring's renewal possible.

Embracing cyclical approaches means collecting fragments in whatever your preferred container is, and experimenting with them until patterns emerge naturally. It might involve voice-recording ideas during pain-free moments or mapping concepts visually, rather than in sequential written outlines. It could mean writing scenes out of order or following your emotions rather than chronology.

When we design our creative practice around our actual minds and bodies, we transform apparent limitations into distinct perspectives. Our stories become more authentic, vivid, and alive. Like wildflowers that thrive in unlikely places, our creativity finds its own path toward the sun. They become more awe-inspiring for having grown through cracks in conventional methods.

ALIGNING PROJECTS WITH OUR EMOTIONAL & PHYSICAL CAPACITY

Aligning our creative work with our actual capacity requires self-trust and flexibility. This means asking what we can realistically do with the energy we have today.

We can explore what formats and tools we can interact with, where our curiosity is leading us, and what would feel amazing to accomplish in the time we can dedicate. This allows us to create with compassion and realistic expectations. With this approach, our stories will bloom in ways we never expected.

Like the first tentative buds of spring, our creative energy ebbs and flows with the seasons of capacity. Some days, we may feel the gentle warmth of inspiration melting away winter's rest and jot down ideas in our creative journals. Other days, our roots may need to remain quietly nourished below the surface by taking in other inspiring works or just living life. Both states are equally valid and necessary for sustainable growth.

Consider how spring gardens accommodate diverse plants. Some flourish in shade, others require full sun, but each grows at their own perfect pace. Similarly, our storytelling practices must honor our unique neurology and embodied experiences. When we force creativity against the natural rhythms of our bodies and minds, we risk depleting the very soil from which our stories grow.

Instead, we can approach our projects with the adaptability of springtime weather. Some days call for the steady drizzle of small, gentle efforts. We might write a single paragraph or make a voice memo capturing a fleeting thought. Other days might bring the unexpected downpour of intense creative flow, where hours pass unnoticed as our stories unfold.

The most vibrant gardens incorporate various heights, textures, and blooming schedules. Your creative practice can embrace similar diversity, using various tools, timeframes, and styles of working that align with your fluctuating capacity.

By trusting the natural seasons of our creative capacity and responding with the same tender care we'd offer newly sprouted seedlings, we cultivate stories that are authentically rooted in our lived experience. Stories that others may recognize as reflections of their own growth journey.

Journal Reflection: *What guides your work most? Emotions? Movement? Inspiration? Talking out projects with a friend? What is one small way you can change your creative time to allow for more of this to increase your capacity to work?*

OUR LIBERATION: Finding Freedom In Project Alignment

When our creative projects align with our deepest needs and values, we discover a profound liberation — like flowers finding their perfect patch of sunshine after a long winter's dormancy. Projects that honor our authentic selves don't deplete us. They replenish our inner landscapes.

This liberation manifests when we release the expectations of conventional productivity and embrace what truly resonates with our unique neurology and embodied wisdom. Our stories become more truthful when they emerge from spaces that accommodate our access needs rather than requiring us to contort ourselves into uncomfortable shapes.

Consider how spring vines grow precisely where they're meant to. Some climb sunward on sturdy trellises. Others sprawl joyfully across garden floors. Similarly, when we allow our creative work to follow the natural contours of our capacity, we're freed from the exhaustion of resistance.

FOLLOWING CURIOSITY RATHER THAN WILLPOWER

When we follow curiosity, we align ourselves with the natural contours of our capacity. Curiosity is like the gentle spring breeze that invites seeds to unfurl at their own pace.

It doesn't demand or force, but beckons us forward with genuine interest and wonder.

Willpower, in contrast, often resembles the harsh methods of forced blooming — applying external pressure and artificial conditions that may yield quick results but ultimately weaken the plant. For neurodivergent and disabled storytellers, relying on willpower typically leads to cycles of burnout, where we push beyond our sustainable limits, collapse, and then berate ourselves for not producing consistently.

Curiosity-led creation honors the winding paths our minds naturally travel. When we notice what fascinates us, such as — what questions wake us at night, what images refuse to leave our thoughts, what stories make our hands itch to write — we tap into an intrinsic motivation that requires significantly less energy to sustain. Our attention flows like rivers following the natural geography of the land.

This approach liberates us from the exhaustion of resistance. Instead of fighting against executive function challenges or fluctuating energy levels, we work with them. On days when traditional writing feels impossible, perhaps we're drawn to research instead, or building character profiles, or dictating dialogue while resting. Each of these curiosity-led activities moves our projects forward organically.

When we surrender to what interests us in each moment, allowing projects to develop through accumulated fascinations rather than forced productivity, we discover a more sustainable creative process. We create systems that respect the seasons of our capacity while still yielding rich and surprising harvests.

There's revolutionary power in creating from this aligned space. Our stories become not just expressions, but embodiments of possibility, showing others that sustainable creativity exists.

MILESTONES THAT HONOR OUR UNIQUE VALUES

It's important for us to begin with reimagining what progress looks like through our own experiential lens. Like a gardener who understands that each plant species has its own definition of thriving, we must develop incremental stepping stones of creative advancement that reflect our authentic needs and capacities.

It is important to question conventional indicators of success. Rather than setting arbitrary word counts or submission deadlines, consider what truly matters within your personal creative ecosystem. Perhaps consistency feels more meaningful than volume, or exploratory drafting brings more joy than polished completion. Your milestones might celebrate maintaining connection with your story during a pain flare, or honor the courage of sharing a vulnerable piece with a trusted friend.

Try translating your values into concrete markers. If accessibility matters deeply, a milestone might be creating an audio version of your work. If community sustains you, perhaps reaching out to fellow disabled storytellers becomes a celebration-worthy achievement. If embodied knowledge guides your practice, acknowledging moments when your writing reflects lived experience becomes a milestone itself.

Document these personalized milestones in a visible way. Create a *flourishing storyteller's growth plan* with blooming flowers representing each achievement, or maintain a growth journal that tracks not just word counts but moments of insight, instances of self-compassion, or days when you honored your body's needs while still nurturing your creative spirit.

Remember that milestones, like spring gardens, should accommodate natural fluctuation. Build flexibility into your expectations. Perhaps create tiered goals for different capacity days. Or celebrate "root system" achievements like research, reflection, rest, alongside more visible "flowering" ones like completed drafts, submissions, publications.

By crafting milestones that reflect your values rather than external expectations, your creative journey becomes not just sustainable but deeply affirming of your whole self.

REWARDS THAT RESTORE

When we complete creative milestones — whether

finishing a draft, working through a difficult scene, or simply showing up to our practice — choosing rewards that genuinely restore us becomes an essential part of sustainable storytelling. Like perennial plants require specific conditions to return season after season, our creative energy needs thoughtful replenishment rather than hollow celebrations.

Consider what truly refills your creative well. For many neurodivergent and disabled storytellers, conventional rewards might actually deplete rather than restore. For instance, instead of noisy social gatherings or overstimulating activities, perhaps you're nourished by a sensory-friendly nature walk or wrapping yourself in a weighted blanket with a cherished book. Or maybe it's savoring a special food that brings comfort and a sensory experience without complications of entertaining company or navigating a crowded restaurant.

Reflect on what the creative process itself gives you beyond the tangible output. Is there relief in finally expressing thoughts that had been circling your mind? Does your imagination provide a welcome respite from physical discomfort? Does capturing your unique perspective validate experiences often missing from mainstream narratives? Recognizing these inherent rewards helps us value the process as much as the final product.

Consider documenting the experience of creation alongside the work itself. Dedicate a page in your creative journal or create a voice memo folder to record how it feels to write that tough scene, what insights emerge unexpectedly, or how your body responds throughout the process. These reflections become valuable data about your creative patterns and needs, while honoring the reality that your feelings and observations are integral parts of the story you're creating.

When you finish the project, you can look back over the journey as you celebrate being done. By choosing rewards that genuinely restore rather than deplete, we cultivate a sustainable relationship with creativity that can weather the changing seasons of our capacity.

Pocket Note: This spring, may your stories grow in ways that honor your body, your mind, and your heart. Every seed you plant—big or small—adds beauty to the world.

PRACTICE: THE FLOURISHING STORYTELLER'S GROWTH PLAN

Your storytelling journey is like tending a garden. Each milestone represents a stage of growth. From planting the first seed of an idea to harvesting the fruits of your storytelling labor, each step matters. Creating this plan will help you track progress in a way that honors your unique creative process.

Step 1: Choose Your Garden Layout
- Grab a sheet of paper and a pencil.
- Take a moment to close your eyes, breathe deeply, and feel inward.
- Where does your creative energy resonate in you?
- Connect with that area of yourself.
- If it were a garden, what shape would it take? Would it be neat little rows of a vegetable garden? A spiral herb garden? A traditional diamond cut flower garden, each corner growing something different?
- Sketch the layout.
- Notice how many separate areas you pictured. Maybe it's one large space. Maybe it's several distinct areas with walking paths between. Maybe it's a patio garden with a bunch of small pots. Each of these is likely a reflection of projects your creative self has percolated.
- Remember that just because you have a dozen areas doesn't mean that all of them are ready to be filled with story seeds this season. It's okay to dream of where future you will expand.

Step 2: Find Your Starting Place
- Identify which is your current creative space. Maybe you've already finished a few projects and have some established areas. Maybe you're just starting out and it's simply a plot of dirt. Many of you will be in

between with a collection of story seeds, some basic tools, and a few test pots where you've started working on growing some stories, but they haven't really taken root. Or they desperately need to be transplanted into the fertile earth, where they can stretch and grow.
- Look at your map and reflect on where you are in your creative journey. Where does your energy want to go? Does it want to collect seeds and germinate them in the greenhouse of your imagination? Is it ready to transplant some seedlings into the soil? Does it want to work on something that is already in the ground, but not thriving?
- Place a stepping stone in front of that area.

Step 3: Establish what is next for you.

What imperfect actions do you need to take this season? Maybe you need to gather tools and learn how to grow stories from an expert gardener. Maybe you need to compost some old ideas and turn over the earth and start a new endeavor. Maybe you need to germinate ideas and plant just one or two in your flower bed. Maybe it's time to prune your rose bush of a novel so it can blossom fully. Or maybe it is time to harvest some of your work and get it to the farmer's market or sell directly to your neighborly readers.

Step 4: Define your boundary markers.

These are what you need to protect your creative space

from the distractions of critters. Consider what things keep you from spending time being creative and experimenting with story?

Maybe you need a tall fence to keep out nosy deer or a brick boundary to keep out the weeds. Create a symbolic physical barrier that symbolizes a real one. For example, a closed gate that symbolizes that you will close your door while working so as not to be disturbed. Or maybe a M shaped border to say you'll protect Mondays from appointments and errands so you can get to your desk with enough spoons to be creative.

Step 5: Create an activity legend

Break down your creative work into small, manageable activities. Use symbols to track progress. Here are a few suggestions, but follow your body's wisdom to decide what you should use.

Flower — Add one small flower in the section you are working on for each small but important win on your projects. For example, brainstorming an idea, creating a character, writing for ten minutes or 100 words, etc. Anything that makes progress.

Water Drop — Use this when you take an action that nurtures your work, but isn't directly adding to it, like researching, revising, sending emails to agents or publishers, putting an ad up to sell your book, or promote your channel, etc.

Sunshine — Add a sunshine anytime you have an "aha"

breakthrough moment. For example, find new inspiration, solve a plot issue, figure out something about a character that helps solidify their goal, motivation, or stakes, etc.

Compost — Add a little spiral or scribble, anytime you learn from a setback and use it to grow stronger.

Step 6: Celebrate Each Bloom/Fruit

Create a list of fun milestones and rewards to recognize your achievements. Reward yourself in ways that feel joyful: stickers, a cozy tea break, a creative treat, or a self-kindness note.

Milestones to celebrate:

In the ground/pot — Small but exciting projects like a poem, short story, or full chapter.

Planting a row of crops — Maybe you see the chapters in your book or scenes in your script in neat little rows. When you finish a draft, you can celebrate.

Well-watered flowers — As you edit and revise, your plants will grow. Celebrate as each one reaches maturity.

Flourishing — Enjoying the creative process. Showing up for several sessions.

Step 7: The Garden of Reflection

Growth takes time, and every stage is valuable. Use the bottom of your map to reflect on:

- What's thriving? (What's going well in your creative journey?)
- What needs more nurturing? (What areas need more attention or care?)

- What are you learning? (Celebrate discoveries and insights.)

CHAPTER 9: When Creating Feels Impossible

"The deep roots never doubt spring will come."
— *Marty Rubin*

THE MYTH: Creative Blocks Mean We are Lazy

WILLPOWER DOESN'T SOLVE EVERYTHING

Perhaps no writing critique is more poisonous than the belief that sufficient willpower can overcome any obstacle.

This idea sends its roots deep into our creative practice, choking out self-compassion and sustainable growth. When we struggle to create, we're told to simply try harder, push through, or force ourselves to sit at our desk until something emerges.

This approach fails to recognize that creativity, like tending a garden, requires the right conditions to flourish. A seed doesn't grow through sheer determination. It requires appropriate soil, water, light, and temperature.

Similarly, our creative capacity exists within the ecosystem of our diverse bodies, minds, and environments. No amount of willpower can make tomatoes grow in frozen soil or coax blossoms from plants that haven't been watered.

For neurodivergent and disabled storytellers, the willpower myth is particularly dangerous because it frames our naturally fluctuating capacity as a moral failing rather than an inherent reality. When we internalize this belief, we exhaust ourselves by cultivating story in conditions that cannot sustain it, further depleting our limited energy reserves and pushing ourselves toward deeper burnout.

IGNORING OUR PHYSICAL & MENTAL BARRIERS

Standard creative advice rarely acknowledges the very real barriers many of us face, both internally and externally. "Write every day" becomes impossible guidance when chronic pain makes sitting upright an achievement. "Just eliminate distractions" dismisses how ADHD brains may actually require certain types of stimulation to focus. "Push through the resistance" disregards how anxiety disorders can trigger debilitating fight-or-flight responses during creative vulnerability.

These traditional approaches assume a neurotypical, able-bodied baseline that simply doesn't exist for many creators. When we fail to thrive under these inappropriate conditions, we're often made to feel as though we lack commitment or are just lazy rather than recognizing that we're trying to grow roses in the desert.

True liberation comes when we acknowledge these barriers as legitimate factors that require accommodation rather than character flaws to overcome. Just as a garden may require raised beds for accessibility or shade cloths to protect delicate plants, our creative practice might need dictation software, body-supporting furniture, medication management, or collaborative approaches that work with our unique needs rather than against them.

THE FALSE DIVIDE BETWEEN "REAL" STORYTELLERS & EVERYONE ELSE

Perhaps most frustrating is the artificial boundary drawn between "real creators" who supposedly produce work consistently regardless of circumstances and everyone else who "just isn't committed enough." This divisive myth suggests there are natural-born artists whose dedication transcends all barriers, and then there's the rest of us, merely playing at creativity.

In reality, creativity exists on a spectrum as diverse as the plant kingdom itself. Some creators may indeed produce work with apparent ease, but this often reflects privilege rather than inherent superiority. They may have access to resources, support systems, or neurological and physical conditions that facilitate consistent production. Others may create in bursts separated by necessary fallow periods, like perennial plants that disappear entirely before emerging again with renewed vigor.

The freedom found in rejecting this false dichotomy is profound. When we understand that all creators — published, acclaimed, struggling, or just beginning — face their own unique hurdles, we free ourselves from the shame of comparison. We recognize that our worth isn't measured by constant productivity but by the authentic expression that emerges when we honor our capacity.

True creativity doesn't require us to transcend our humanity but to embrace it fully, with all its limitations and possibilities. Like a garden that accommodates diverse growing conditions, our creative community flourishes most when we validate multiple paths to expression rather than enforcing a single, narrow definition of what it means to be a "real" storyteller.

THE TRUTH: Creative Barriers Are Complex

THE LINK BETWEEN LACK OF REST & CREATIVE BLOCKS

What we interpret as creative blocks often represent our body and mind's innate wisdom calling for necessary rest and nourishment. Like a garden that appears dormant in winter, our creative capacity isn't absent — it's conserving energy for future growth. When we experience resistance to creating stories, this may be the internal equivalent of soil requiring rejuvenation before it can support new life.

The relentless pace of capitalist productivity has taught us to view rest as laziness rather than as an essential part of the creative cycle. Yet in nature, we see how fallow periods are crucial for sustained abundance. Fields left unplanted for a season return with renewed fertility. Trees that appear lifeless in winter burst with blossoms in spring. Our creative capacity follows similar rhythms. Periods of output naturally alternate with periods of input and restoration.

For storytellers like us, honoring this link between rest and creativity becomes not only beneficial but essential. Stepping away from active story isn't abandoning our practice, it sustains it. The greatest act of creative courage might be allowing our gardens to lie dormant when needed, trusting that beneath the surface, important processes continue. That ideas are composting, inspiration is germinating, and creative energy will slowly replenish itself for when conditions again support growth.

THE CHALLENGES OF CREATING WITH DIVERSE BRAINS & BODIES

Creating stories while navigating diverse neurological and physical experiences presents unique challenges. Just as gardens must be adapted for different climate zones, soil types, and available sunlight, our creative practices require environments and approaches tailored to our specific needs.

For those with executive function differences, the seemingly simple task of beginning a project can feel like trying to coax seedlings from frozen ground. Sensory processing differences might make standard work environments as hostile to concentration as attempting to garden in a windstorm. Chronic pain or fatigue might limit working time to brief intervals, requiring us to nurture projects in small patient increments rather than marathon sessions.

The freedom in acknowledging these realities lies not in resignation, but in adaptation. We can liberate ourselves by experimenting with modified tools and methods. Perhaps our garden needs wider pathways for easier access, or specialized tools that accommodate limited dexterity. Perhaps our creative practice thrives with dictation software instead of typing, collaborative approaches that provide structure, or permission to work in micro-sessions that honor energy limitations.

By reimagining creative practice as adaptable rather than rigid, we discover that barriers aren't evidence of creative inadequacy. They are invitations to innovative approaches that enhance our unique artistic voice.

PAUSES & BOREDOM ARE PART OF THE CREATIVE PROCESS

In the natural world, periods of apparent inactivity are when essential transformations occur. Pollination happens in brief, sometimes invisible moments. Fruit ripens at its own perfect pace. Similarly, what appears as creative pauses or boredom often masks the subtle, necessary work of our unconscious mind processing experiences, connecting disparate ideas, and preparing for new growth.

Our culture's discomfort with boredom has led us to fill every moment with stimulation. This leaves little space for the wandering mind that generates unexpected connections. Yet many breakthrough ideas emerge not during active work but in the shower, on walks, or while engaged in routine tasks that allow our attention to drift.

These pauses aren't interruptions to creativity, but essential components.

For neurodivergent and disabled storytellers especially, these fallow periods may appear differently than expected. What looks like distraction — following seemingly unrelated interests, diving into research rabbit holes, or shifting between multiple projects — frequently serves as the cross-pollination that eventually enriches our work.

When we embrace pauses, we release the pressure of constant, visible productivity. When we understand that creativity includes periods of dormancy, we can trust the unseen processes happening beneath the surface.

Like a garden in its seasonal cycles, our creative practice includes necessary phases of rest, integration, and seemingly random exploration. All of these fertilize the flowers for when new ideas finally form and delicious fruit is produced.

Pauses in creativity aren't a sign that we've lost our spark. They're a time of incubation, where ideas quietly grow. Boredom and stillness lead to breakthroughs. Recognizing the value of these still periods allows us to embrace the full spectrum of our creative experience.

Journal Reflection: *When do your best ideas come? What activities pollinate your work? How can you incorporate these before your creative time in your week?*

OUR LIBERATION: Staying Creative Beyond Output

Liberating ourselves from the myth of laziness means recognizing that creativity is not just about producing finished works. It's about nurturing our imaginations, connecting with our ideas, and valuing the process itself. Here are ways to stay creatively engaged, even when creating feels impossible.

ACCEPTING WHERE YOU ARE RIGHT NOW

The first step toward liberation is accepting your current reality without judgment. Just as a gardener must work with the actual soil and climate conditions rather than an idealized version, we must honor our authentic capacity.

Give yourself permission to rest without guilt. Rest is not the opposite of creativity. It's part of it. In nature, dormancy is an essential phase of growth. Seeds require darkness and stillness before germination. Plants conserve energy during winter. The soil replenishes nutrients during fallow periods.

Similarly, our creative capacity needs withdrawal and restoration to remain sustainable. These quiet periods aren't failures, but necessary phases in your creative cycle.

Name and validate your current state. "I'm in a resting phase." Or "my creativity is incubating" can shift your mindset from frustration to self-compassion. Language shapes our perception of experience. When we reframe periods of lower output as legitimate parts of the creative process rather than deficiencies, we release the shame that often accompanies them. This simple act of naming can transform what feels like creative drought into recognized creative dormancy.

Trust that your creativity will return. Like spring after winter, stories bloom when they're ready. Our creative energy follows natural rhythms that don't always align with external expectations or schedules. For neurodivergent and disabled storytellers, these rhythms may be particularly unpredictable, influenced by health fluctuations, medication changes, or varying access needs. Trusting the cyclical nature of creativity means recognizing that periods of apparent inactivity often precede surprising bursts of insight or inspiration.

This trust isn't passive resignation, but active faith in your creative nature. It acknowledges that creativity is innate to human experience. Not a scarce resource that might be permanently depleted, but a renewable capacity that exists even when temporarily inaccessible. Just as the underground root systems of perennial plants remain alive beneath winter soil, your creative foundations persist during dormant periods.

VALUING PASSIVE CREATIVE WORK

Much of what nurtures creativity happens beneath the surface, invisible to productivity metrics but essential to the ecosystem of imagination.

Give yourself credit for thinking about your story, even if you aren't actively writing. The mental exploration of character motivations, plot possibilities, or thematic connections is legitimate creative work. For those with executive function differences or physical limitations that make active writing challenging, this inner development can constitute the majority of creative engagement. It deserves recognition as such.

It's also important to enjoy media that resonates with your project. Movies, books, music, and podcasts can act as creative fuel. Consumption is not the opposite of creation, but is often a necessary precursor. When we engage thoughtfully with others' creative works, we're collecting seeds for our own gardens — gathering imagery, cadences, emotional textures, and conceptual frameworks that nourish our imaginations.

Daydream freely. Let your imagination wander without expectation or structure. Daydreaming is often devalued in productivity-focused cultures. But it's actually a sophisticated cognitive process that allows for unusual connections and insights. For neurodivergent thinkers especially, these unstructured thought journeys can yield surprising creative pathways that more linear approaches might miss. Honor these meandering explorations as valuable creative territory.

This validation of passive creativity matters for those navigating chronic illness or disability, where energy for active creation may be limited. Recognizing that you're still engaged with your creative practice, even during periods of rest, reinforces that creativity isn't contingent on constant production. It exists as an ongoing relationship with your imagination.

SHIFTING OUR FOCUS FROM PRODUCTION TO PROCESS

When we value process over product, we discover liberation from external metrics of success and reconnect with intrinsic creative joy.

Create for the sake of exploration, not completion. Let go of timelines or goals when necessary. Approach your creative practice as an expedition into unknown territory rather than a journey toward a predetermined destination. This exploratory mindset allows for discovery, surprise, and organic development — experiences often sacrificed when we focus exclusively on finishing.

Try experimenting with low-pressure formats like journaling, doodling, or making voice notes. These informal approaches reduce the internal critic that often accompanies more structured creative work. They invite playfulness and imperfection, creating safe spaces to experiment without consequence.

For those with perfectionist tendencies or anxiety, these formats can bypass the pressure associated with "real" writing and allow creative energy to flow more freely.

Notice any sparks of joy or curiosity, no matter how small. Those are signs of creative energy at work. The moment of satisfaction when you find precisely the right word, the curiosity piqued by an unexpected character decision, the pleasant surprise of a metaphor that connects seemingly unrelated concepts — these flickers of engagement are worth celebrating. They indicate that your creative spirit remains active, even if its expression looks different than expected.

This process-oriented approach transforms creativity from achievement into presence — from something you accomplish to something you experience. For those with chronic illness or disability, where consistent progress toward completion may be challenging, this shift allows for meaningful creative engagement regardless of output.

FINDING ACCOUNTABILITY PARTNERS

Community can provide both motivation and validation when creating feels difficult, but the quality of these connections matters deeply.

It's important to connect with fellow storytellers who understand your experiences. Gentle check-ins and shared creative time can be encouraging. Find companions who recognize the complexities of creating while navigating neurodivergence, chronic illness, or disability. They should be people who understand fluctuating capacity, accessibility needs, and non-linear progress. These understanding partners can provide validation that generic writing groups might not offer.

Choose partners who celebrate effort and curiosity, not just results. The ideal creative companion recognizes the courage in showing up for your practice, regardless of how much you produce.

Encourage them to ask, "What interested you today?" rather than "How many pages did you write?" They should understand that maintaining a connection to your creativity during difficult periods is itself an achievement worth honoring.

Create together without pressure. Co-writing sessions, creative hangouts, or a quiet virtual coworking can help you feel less alone. The simple presence of others engaged in their own creative practices can provide motivation without competition. These shared spaces acknowledge that creativity thrives in community — that we don't have to choose between connection and creation but can nurture both simultaneously.

These thoughtfully chosen creative relationships can transform potential isolation into collaborative growth. Like companion planting in a garden, where certain species support and enhance each other, the right creative partners amplify your natural strengths while providing support for your challenges.

By accepting your current reality, valuing invisible creative work, focusing on process over product, and finding supportive community, we reclaim creativity as an inherent aspect of our humanity rather than a productivity metric. This liberation allows our creative practice to become not another source of depletion but a sustainable wellspring of meaning, connection, and authentic expression, regardless of how much we visibly produce.

PRACTICE: EASY CREATIVE PROMPTS FOR DIFFICULT DAYS

- **Five Senses Check-In:** Describe what you see, hear, smell, taste, and feel in your current environment. Let those details inspire a short scene or memory.
- **Character Letters:** Write a letter to or from one of your characters, even if it's unrelated to your main story.

- **Mood Boards:** Gather images, colors, and textures that capture the feeling of your story world.
- **Dialogue Snippets:** Imagine a conversation between your characters and jot down their voices without worrying about the plot.

Pocket Note: You are not lazy. Your creativity is still alive, even when it feels dormant. By tending to your needs and honoring your unique process, you are growing something beautiful. Trust that your stories will bloom in their own time.

CHAPTER 10: Healing Our Stories

"The promise of spring's arrival is enough to get anyone through the bitter winter." — Jen Selinsky

THE MYTH: Creation Is About Publication, Recognition, & Profit

EXTERNAL SUCCESS AS THE MEASURE OF VALUE

For neurodivergent, chronically ill, and disabled storytellers, the dominant narrative often frames creativity as something that only matters if it leads to publication, recognition, or financial success. The myth says our stories must be marketable to be valuable, and they are only worth celebrating when they earn external validation.

This perspective overshadows our creative practice, like an invasive species that gradually chokes out native growth. We question the worth of projects that bring us joy but might not appeal to mainstream audiences. We hesitate to celebrate small victories if they don't align with conventional milestones that others will celebrate with us. We dismiss our most authentic work when it doesn't fit neatly into marketable genres or formats.

The pressure to achieve external validation creates a harsh environment for those whose creative energy fluctuates with their health or access needs. When publication timelines, promotional responsibilities, or networking expectations don't accommodate our embodied realities, we conclude that we're not cut out for creative work. When, in reality, the system is designed without us in mind.

This myth withers our innate creativity, training us to evaluate potential projects not by their resonance with our authentic voice but by their projected commercial viability. Like judging a garden solely on which plants could stock a produce stand rather than which ones thrive in our particular soil, we limit what we allow ourselves to grow.

CREATIVITY MUST HAVE A MARKETABLE PURPOSE

The belief that creativity must serve a marketable purpose stems from our culture's discomfort with activities that exist purely for their own sake. Wildflowers are often dismissed as weeds because they can't be sold at the market. So too are creative pursuits with no commercial application devalued as frivolous or indulgent.

This perspective transforms creation from a natural human behavior into another arena where we must optimize, compete, and produce measurable outcomes. Suddenly, our stories aren't expressions of our humanity but products to be evaluated, packaged, and sold. Our writing practice isn't a source of connection or meaning, but a potential revenue stream that must justify the resources it consumes.

For those whose energy and focus are already limited, this pressure to monetize adds an unnecessary burden to our creative process. Instead of following our curiosity or honoring our unique perspective, we find ourselves second-guessing whether a project is "worth pursuing" based on its market potential rather than its personal significance.

The irony is that this market-driven approach often produces work that is less distinctive, less authentic, and ultimately less compelling, even by commercial standards. Just as monoculture farming depletes soil of its natural diversity and resilience, creativity cultivated solely for market appeal tends to lose the very uniqueness that might have made it valuable.

MARKET-DRIVEN WORK MISSES CREATIVITY'S HEALING POWER

But storytelling is not just about producing sellable work. It is a form of self-expression. A way to make sense of our experiences, and a tool for connection. For those of us navigating the complexities of chronic illness and neurodivergence, the act of creation itself can be deeply healing — whether or not anyone else ever reads our words.

This healing power exists independent of publication or profit. When we write our experiences, we externalize what might otherwise remain locked within us. When we craft fictional worlds, we create spaces where we have agency that chronic illness or disability might limit in our physical reality. When we play with language, we engage in a form of sensory pleasure that can provide relief from pain or overwhelm.

These therapeutic aspects of creativity operate regardless of commercial viability. Like medicinal herbs growing freely in untended corners of the garden, they offer their benefits without requiring cultivation for market purposes. The quieter story that helps us process our diagnosis may never see publication, but might be precisely what we need to write. The experimental poem that captures our sensory experience might not fit commercial publishing categories, but could be essential to expressing our unique perspective.

Capitalist systems that prioritize output over experience reinforce this belief. Creativity is often seen as a product, not a process. Platforms are saturated with messages that encourage us to monetize our hobbies, optimize our work, and hustle harder. When we struggle to keep up with these expectations, we internalize the idea that we are not "real" storytellers.

Liberation comes when we recognize this myth for what it is — a narrative that serves markets rather than creators. Instead, we must reclaim creativity as an inherent human right rather than a commercial endeavor. We must free ourselves to create the work that truly matters to us. Like tending a garden for the joy of growing rather than the profit of selling, we can write for the pleasure, healing, connection, and meaning it brings to our lives.

This doesn't mean publication or recognition aren't valid desires. They can be wonderful outcomes of our creative work. But when they become the primary measure of value, we sacrifice the very aspects of creativity that might sustain us through the challenges of disability and illness. Things such as story's capacity to comfort, to make meaning, to connect, and to celebrate our unique ways of experiencing the world.

THE TRUTH: Stories Heal & Liberate

STORYTELLING AS AN ANCIENT HEALING PRACTICE

Storytelling has always been a source of healing. Across cultures and histories, stories have been used to process grief, celebrate joy, and make meaning out of uncertainty. When we write, we are engaging in an ancient practice of turning our inner worlds into something tangible.

This alchemical process of transforming intangible experience into concrete expression creates a bridge between our internal landscape and the external world. For those of us navigating chronic illness, disability, or neurodivergence, this bridge becomes vital. Our experiences often exist in realms difficult for others to access or understand. Explaining our invisible pain, sensory overwhelm, cognitive fog, and unpredictable energy fluctuations can best be done with story. Through creative expression, we render these experiences visible, giving form to what might otherwise remain unseen.

The act of shaping narrative from chaos offers a unique

form of control. When illness or disability introduces unpredictability into our lives, the page becomes territory where we determine the boundaries.

We decide which aspects of experience to magnify, which to transform through metaphor, which to set aside. This sovereignty over our stories provides a counterbalance to medical systems that often reduce us to symptoms or diagnostic codes.

Writing also creates a record that persists beyond moments of wellness or capacity. On days when brain fog descends or fatigue limits our ability to function, our previously written words stand as evidence of our complex inner lives. They remind us that our identity extends beyond current limitations. That we contain multitudes beyond what any single day might reveal.

CREATIVE EXPRESSION AS RESISTANCE TO ABLEIST CULTURE

For neurodivergent and disabled storytellers, creativity offers a way to reclaim agency. In a world that defines our worth by our productivity, creating simply for the sake of expression remains an act of resistance. It allows us to tell stories that challenge ableist narratives, celebrate our complexities, and offer perspectives that are too often silenced.

By writing our experiences, we counter the medical and

cultural narratives that position disability as either tragedy or inspiration. We articulate the nuances of lived experience that clinical language cannot capture. We share the unexpected gifts alongside genuine struggles, the humor that coexists with hardship, the insights gained through navigating worlds not designed for our bodies or minds.

Creative expression also allows us to reimagine accessibility. When traditional publishing or artistic spaces exclude us through physical barriers, inflexible deadlines, or narrow aesthetic standards, we can create alternative pathways. Digital platforms, collaborative projects, and community publishing initiatives offer possibilities for sharing our work outside conventional systems. Through these channels, we not only make our own voices heard, but create openings for others whose stories have been similarly marginalized.

This resistance extends to the very rhythms of our creative practice. By honoring body-based timelines rather than arbitrary deadlines, by measuring progress in moments of authentic expression rather than word counts or publication credits, we model alternatives to capitalist productivity metrics. Each time we validate slow creation, intermittent work patterns, or unconventional approaches, we chip away at systems that have defined creativity too narrowly.

FINDING DEEP MEANING IN SMALL CREATIVE FRAGMENTS

Even small creative acts, like a few lines of poetry, a voice memo capturing a passing thought, a daydream explored on paper, can hold immense power. These fragments may never become traditional "finished" projects, but they are no less valuable. They are evidence of our inner lives, of our resilience and imagination.

For those with fluctuating energy or cognitive capacity, these fragments constitute the majority of our creative output. A single metaphor crafted during a pain flare might represent greater creative courage than a chapter written during ease. A brief character sketch dictated between medical appointments might contain more authentic truth than a polished essay produced under pressure.

These creative moments function as touchstones — small but significant markers of our continuing engagement with life and meaning. Like the first green shoots emerging after winter, they remind us that our creative capacity remains alive even during dormant periods. They demonstrate that creativity doesn't require grand gestures or complete narratives to be meaningful.

When collected over time, these fragments often reveal patterns and preoccupations we might not otherwise recognize. The recurring images, the persistent questions, the themes that emerge across scattered notes become a map of our inner territory. They show us what matters to us, what puzzles us, what we continue to work through across months or years of creative engagement.

By honoring these fragments as complete in themselves rather than mere stepping stones to "real" projects, we further liberate ourselves from externally imposed standards of creative value. We recognize that sometimes the smallest seed contains everything necessary for growth, even if that growth follows timelines invisible to others. In recognizing this truth lies profound self-compassion that can sustain our creative practice through all seasons of capacity.

Journal Reflection: *Find one fragment and reflect on the lessons that it has taught you.*

OUR LIBERATION: Storytelling for Liberation

Liberating ourselves from the myth of market-driven creativity means embracing storytelling as a practice of self-care and self-discovery. Below are some ways to explore storytelling as medicine, honoring your needs and experiences.

CREATING AS A TOOL FOR

PROCESSING EXPERIENCES

When we approach storytelling as medicine, we recognize its power to help us metabolize tough experiences and celebrate moments of joy. Like plants transforming sunlight into nourishment, our creativity transforms raw experience into meaning.

One way to do this is to write letters you never send. Let your emotions pour out without worrying about structure or polish. These private communications can be to your younger self, to your illness, or to those who've hurt or helped you. These create safe containers for processing complex feelings. The page becomes a witness that holds your anger, grief, gratitude, or confusion without judgment or interruption.

You can also journal through difficult moments, using prompts like: "What would this experience say if it had a voice?" or "What story am I telling myself about this situation?" By externalizing internal narratives, we create distance that allows for new perspectives. The act of naming what we're experiencing helps transform the overwhelming sensations into navigable territory.

Another option is to explore speculative storytelling to imagine new possibilities. What would healing look like in a fantastical world? How might your future self offer comfort or wisdom? Fiction allows us to experiment with alternate realities and outcomes without the limitations of our current circumstances. Through metaphor and imagination, we discover what might be possible beyond the constraints of medical prognoses or societal expectations.

When we're navigating chronic illness or disability, our narratives are often medicalized, reduced to symptoms and treatments. Creative expression returns the storytelling power to our hands, allowing us to integrate these experiences into the broader tapestry of our lives. Through writing, we remind ourselves that we are more than our diagnoses. We are meaning-makers, pattern-seekers, and storytellers.

WRITING NEW NARRATIVES ABOUT DISABILITY & DIFFERENCE

Traditional narratives about disability often fall into limited tropes, such as the inspirational overcomer, the tragic victim, the bitter antagonist. By creating our own stories, we cultivate a more nuanced garden of representation.

We must reclaim the narrative by writing stories that center disabled and neurodivergent experiences. We must create characters who reflect our truths. When we position disability and neurodivergence as central rather than peripheral, we challenge the assumption that our experiences are deviations from a presumed "normal." Our protagonist's sensory sensitivities, mobility aids, or communication differences can be woven into the fabric of the story without becoming its sole focus.

We can also challenge harmful tropes by exploring complex, joyful, and empowered representations of disability in our work. Show characters navigating interdependence rather than emphasizing only independence. Depict access needs as natural rather than burdensome. Celebrate adaptive creativity and community care. These representations not only counter damaging stereotypes, but offer possibilities for how we might view our own experiences.

It is important to write from the body. Notice how your physical experiences shape your creativity. Allow pain, joy, fatigue, or sensory experiences to guide your storytelling. Rather than trying to transcend the body in pursuit of some disembodied "perfect" creativity, embrace how your particular embodiment informs your unique perspective. The ways you perceive the world—through chronic pain, sensory differences, mobility variations—provide insights and angles unavailable to others.

This embodied writing becomes particularly powerful when shared with others navigating similar experiences. Finding yourself reflected in another's words can be profoundly validating, a reminder that you are not alone in your experiences. Your stories, when shared, become part of a larger ecosystem of disability narratives that nurture collective understanding and growth.

HARMFUL IDEAS ABOUT THE CREATIVE PROCESS

Conventional wisdom about creativity frequently emphasizes discipline, consistency, and completion. These qualities may be at odds with fluctuating capacity or executive function differences.

We can counter this by releasing the pressure to finish every project. Allow yourself to write fragments, sketches, and incomplete pieces without judgment. These creative seedlings have value even if they never grow into full-sized plants. They capture moments of insight, preserve fleeting emotions, and keep your creative channels open during periods when larger projects feel overwhelming.

Trust that every story you create, no matter how small, has meaning. The process is just as valuable as the result. When we focus exclusively on outcomes, we miss the insights, pleasures, and discoveries that emerge during creation itself. The joy of finding exactly the right metaphor, the relief of expressing a long-held feeling, the surprise of an unexpected character voice matter regardless of whether they result in a finished piece.

Finally, redefine success on your own terms. Success might look like finding clarity through writing, feeling pride in your imagination, or simply enjoying a moment of creative play. By establishing criteria that honor your actual experiences rather than external metrics, you create sustainable motivation that can weather fluctuations in capacity.

CREATING FROM OUR BODIES, NOT DESPITE THEM

Our creative practices often assume certain bodily capacities. When we adapt these practices to our actual bodies, we discover new pathways to expression.

Give yourself permission to dictate stories if typing is difficult, use visual art or collage to capture emotions, or take mindful storytelling walks. These adaptations aren't compromises but innovations that enhance your creative voice. Dictation captures the natural rhythms of spoken language. Visual approaches bypass verbal blocks. Movement integrates body wisdom into your storytelling.

This allows you to embrace your natural rhythms. Some days may be for imagining, others for drafting, still others for resting. Each stage is part of the creative cycle. Remember, just as gardens have seasons of planting, growth, harvest, and fallow periods, our creativity follows natural ebbs and flows. By honoring our rhythms rather than fighting against them, we conserve precious energy and align our creative practice with our capacity.

Let go of comparisons. Your process is beautifully unique. It will not look like anyone else's. The conditions of your life, body, and mind shape your creative approach just as specific soil conditions determine what will thrive in a particular garden. The adaptations, workarounds, and innovations you develop are specialized tools that help your creativity flourish in its particular environment.

Through these practices, storytelling becomes not another demand on our limited energy but a source of renewal. It's a place where we can process, imagine, and create on our own terms. This liberation from market-driven creativity allows our stories to grow naturally from the rich soil of our lived experience, nourishing both ourselves and others who encounter them.

Pocket Note: Storytelling is not something we have to master. It's something we get to experience. Let your stories grow, shift, and bloom in their own time. In this act of creation, you are tending to yourself—and that is more than enough.

CHAPTER 11: Preparing for Summer's Intensity

"Spring work is going on with joyful enthusiasm."
— John Muir

THE MYTH: We Should Enter Summer Full Throttle

As spring yields to summer, we face a critical transition that demands our attention and care. For neurodivergent, chronically ill, and disabled storytellers, this shift isn't simply about changing wardrobes or updating playlists. It fundamentally alters how our bodies and minds function, how we create, and how we sustain ourselves.

This pervasive belief has trapped many of us in cycles of burnout and disappointment. Society celebrates those who "make the most" of summer, who maintain or even increase their creative output despite rising temperatures, shifting routines, and new physical demands. Today, we liberate ourselves from this harmful expectation.

THE EXPECTATION OF SEAMLESS SEASONAL TRANSITIONS

We've been conditioned to believe that seasons should flow one into another without disruption to our productivity or creative processes. Magazines and social media perpetuate images of effortless transitions. This season starts with spring cleaning that whisks away the stale energy of winter. It ends with high energy flowing perfectly into summer adventures, all while maintaining consistent work output.

But our bodies know better. They register each degree of temperature change, each shift in barometric pressure, each additional hour of daylight. For those with chronic pain, temperature sensitivity, or sensory processing differences, these changes aren't background noise. They're foreground demands requiring significant adaptation.

The truth is liberating. Seasonal transitions require

intentional adjustment periods. Just as we wouldn't expect a garden to instantly adapt to summer's intensity without proper preparation, we cannot demand this of ourselves.

HOW STANDARD ADVICE OVERLOOKS SEASONAL EFFECTS

"Drink more water." "Get up earlier to beat the heat." "Use summer's energy boost for your creative projects."

These well-intended suggestions overlook the complex reality of how seasonal changes affect diverse bodies and minds. Standard productivity advice rarely acknowledges how heat can exacerbate chronic pain. How longer days can disrupt carefully balanced sleep schedules. How changing routines deeply impacts those who rely on predictability.

Our liberation comes in recognizing these oversights. When we acknowledge that standard advice often fails us, we create space to develop personalized approaches that honor our unique needs. We can see clearly that one-size-fits-all seasonal advice was never designed for bodies and minds like ours.

THE PRESSURE TO MAINTAIN CONSTANT OUTPUT

Summer's intensity often requires us to shift how we work. We may need to write in shorter bursts, change what time of day we work, or alter what we work on. These aren't compromises or failures. They're sophisticated adaptations to our changing environment.

With eyes wide open, we recognize this pressure for what it is — an artificial construct that disregards both our wellbeing and nature's example. Just as even the most abundant garden doesn't produce the same crops year-round, our creative work must shift with the seasons.

THE TRUTH: Thoughtful Transitions Protect Creativity

Transitioning from spring's gentle growth into summer's intensity is an opportunity to reassess our needs. Rather than forcing ourselves to meet external expectations, we can thoughtfully manage our energy and creativity. This approach honors our bodies and sustains our creative spirit.

Seasons of rest are just as important as seasons of output. When we allow ourselves to pause and reflect, we create space for creative renewal. By tending to our energy with care, we prevent burnout and build resilience.

BUILDING CLEAR BOUNDARIES FOR SUMMER

Just as the gardens we've cultivated require defined boundaries to thrive, our creative practices need clear parameters as we transition to summer.

Consider the following as the seasons change:

- **Morning Temperature Mapping:** Track when your space becomes uncomfortably warm each day for a week before summer begins. This creates a personalized heat timeline, allowing you to shift creative work to cooler hours without waiting until you're already depleted.

- **Energy Forecasting:** Like weather forecasting, this practice involves anticipating your energy fluctuations through summer's progression. Document past patterns if available or establish baseline measurements this season. This ritual replaces surprise with preparation.

- **Creative Container Resizing:** Deliberately adjust your creative expectations to match summer's realities. This might mean shorter writing sessions, different creative mediums, or projects that accommodate inconsistent energy. The container changes, not your commitment to creativity.

- **Sensory Preparation:** Gradually introduce summer's sensory experiences before they become overwhelming. This might include brief exposure to fans or air conditioning sounds, adapting to changing light patterns, or testing cooling tools before they become necessities.

These boundaries aren't limitations. They're liberating

structures that enable sustainable creativity through challenging seasons.

ENTERING SUMMER WITH EYES WIDE OPEN

Previous summers may have caught us unprepared, leaving us depleted as we attempted to maintain unchanged routines in changed conditions. But now we have a different way to approach. We can identify the patterns that have harmed us. We recognize the false narratives we once believed.

Our sovereignty comes when we prepare realistically for summer's intensity. Preparation isn't pessimism, it's profound self-respect. We now understand that adjusting our expectations isn't giving up, but strategic wisdom.

We no longer need to diminish our creative lives. Instead, we protect them. We don't reduce our impact, we ensure it continues. We don't abandon our stories, we create sustainable conditions for them to flourish in new ways.

As spring concludes, we stand at this threshold with clarity and purpose, ready to transition with intention rather than default. This is how we truly honor the stories we carry and the bodies that carry them.

Journal Reflection: Reflect on the lessons spring offered. What surprised you in your creative process? What sparked joy or curiosity? Acknowledge growth beyond the tangible. Emotional insights, small acts of self-compassion, and moments of inspiration are worth celebrating.

OUR LIBERATION: Setting Boundaries for Creative Well-being

Liberation arrives when we recognize we're not obligated to meet unrealistic standards. Our needs are valid, and our creative practices can adapt to support our well-being. For storytellers like us, this freedom is particularly powerful as summer approaches.

Setting creative boundaries doesn't limit our potential, but creates sustainable conditions for our work to thrive despite environmental challenges. These boundaries become protective barriers against burnout, allowing our creativity to flow in ways that honor our bodies rather than exploiting them. By recognizing that adaptation isn't compromise but wisdom, we reframe our entire relationship with creative work.

This liberation extends beyond individual practice to challenge broader narratives about productivity and value. In claiming space for our unique creative rhythms, we reject ableist expectations that measure worth through consistent output. Our boundaries become not just personal tools, but political statements about whose bodies and creative processes are valid and valuable.

HONORING YOUR BODY'S UNIQUE SEASONAL NEEDS & BOUNDARIES

Your body holds wisdom about seasonal transitions that no productivity expert or writing guide can match. Begin by developing a practice of attentive listening to how your body responds to increasing temperatures, longer daylight hours, and changing atmospheric conditions. Track not only obvious symptoms but subtle shifts in your creative thinking, emotional landscape, and sensory processing as spring yields to summer.

This listening practice transforms vague discomfort into actionable information. Perhaps you discover that your cognitive processing slows after temperatures reach a certain level, or that your pain increases with humidity changes. These insights aren't limitations, but valuable data that informs how you structure your creative practice during the summer months.

With this knowledge, reimagine your creative goals through the lens of seasonal adaptation. This might mean shifting from output-based metrics, like finishing three chapters, to process-focused intentions, such as engaging with your story world twice a week. Allow your expectations to flex with your energy. Recognize that consistency might look different in summer than it did in spring.

Prioritize creating environments that support your specific sensory and physical needs during heat increases. This boundary-setting isn't selfish, but a necessary stewardship of your creative capacity during challenging conditions.

DEVELOPING STRATEGIES FOR HEAT & ENERGY MANAGEMENT

The intensity of summer demands intentional energy management strategies that protect your creative resources. Try mapping the natural rhythms of both your living space and your body throughout the latter days of spring. Identify when temperatures peak in your workspace and when your body experiences the greatest comfort and discomfort.

Using temporal mapping, you can schedule creative sessions during natural windows of opportunity, like early morning hours when both mind and environment remain cool.

Incorporate regular physiological support practices that address summer's specific impacts on your system. For some, this means gentle movement rituals that prevent stiffness from air conditioning or to reduce heat-related inflammation. For others, it involves deliberate nervous system regulation through breathwork or grounding exercises that counter the stimulating effects of increased daylight and temperature.

Transform your creative environment with deliberate attention to sensory needs that intensify during the summer. This might involve creating microclimate zones with strategically placed fans, cooling cloths applied to pulse points during writing sessions, or visual cues that psychologically counter the heat's effects. Consider how sound, light, temperature, and texture interact in your space, making adjustments that reduce the energy tax of sensory processing during creative work.

These strategies aren't makeshift accommodations but sophisticated responses to real environmental conditions. Creativity flourishes when we honor rather than override our physical realities.

SIMPLE END-OF-SPRING RITUALS FOR VARIOUS ENERGY LEVELS

Transition rituals ease change by providing a structure to delineate endings and beginnings. For storytellers with fluctuating energy, these rituals must be accessible across various capacity levels while still providing meaningful closure to spring's creative cycle.

In the final days of spring, when energy runs lowest, engage in gentle reflection practices that require minimal output. Journal a single paragraph about what your creative practice has taught you this season. Or record brief videos capturing impressions rather than structured thoughts.

These micro-reflections honor your journey without demanding energy you may not have. Celebrate what emerged in your garden, whether finished products or moments of engagement. Recognize how you showed up creatively.

If you have moderate energy available, celebrate organization rituals that created clarity and how to use them for summer's work. Gather scattered notes into a single document, revisit half-finished projects with curiosity rather than judgment, and consciously release ideas that no longer resonate. This clearing creates both physical and mental space for whatever summer brings, removing the subtle energy drain of creative clutter.

When energy allows, develop a flexible creative roadmap for summer months. Unlike rigid plans that once set you up for disappointment, this roadmap should identify which projects generate genuine excitement for you. Establish gentle intentions rather than deadlines. And most importantly, deliberately incorporate space for rest, adaptation, and unexpected detours to take side trips following your inspiration. This planning ritual acknowledges both your creative desires and the reality of summer's challenges, creating a framework that supports rather than constrains.

PRACTICE: PREPARE FOR SUMMER WITHOUT SURRENDERING CREATIVE AUTONOMY

Late spring requires conscious preparation for the different energies of summer while protecting the sovereign creative practices you've established.

- **Season Transition Inventory:** Assess your projects, practices, and needs as you move toward summer's different energy and rhythms. Identify which creative elements should continue, which need to adapt, and which need to be released.
- **Heat Adaptation Planning:** Develop specific modifications to your creative practice for summer's physical and energetic challenges. Create alternative workflows for high-temperature days, energy-intensive periods, or changed schedules.
- **Sovereignty Preservation:** Identify aspects of your creative practice most vulnerable to disruption during seasonal transition. Establish protective rituals and boundaries that maintain your creative autonomy through changing conditions.
- **Resource Allocation:** Reassess your creative resources (time, energy, attention, space, materials, support) in light of summer's approaching demands. Plan to allocate your resources in ways that protect your most essential creative work.

By approaching this transition intentionally, you can maintain agency over your creative practice rather than surrendering to external seasonal pressures.

FAREWELL: Our Ongoing Journey

"The pleasures of spring are available to everybody, and cost nothing." — George Orwell

Resisting the myth of instant and persistent creation is an act of self-care. Each season offers new lessons, and by honoring our own rhythms, we free ourselves from harmful expectations. As spring arrives, know that your creativity remains valid whether it blooms boldly or quietly rests.

The experimental nature of spring's awakening invites us to approach our creative practice with renewed curiosity.

Like seedlings testing the warming soil, we too can emerge in ways uniquely suited to our particular conditions. Our creative gardens don't need to question whether the crocus belongs alongside the late-blooming dahlia, or if the shade-loving fern deserves its place as much as the sun-seeking marigold. Each of our stories can follow its own timeline and thrive in conditions that honor its inherent nature.

As neurodivergent, chronically ill, and disabled storytellers, we are similarly diverse in our needs and expressions. Our creative journeys may follow winding paths rather than straight lines. We can use specialized tools, adaptive environments, or collaborative approaches with confidence. We can radically accept that our work will emerge in rhythms different from those we've been taught. This diversity of approach doesn't diminish the value of our stories. It enhances them and brings perspectives to the literary landscape that have too long been missing.

Remember that even the most established gardens require ongoing experimentation. Conditions change, unexpected frosts occur, new pests arrive, and previously thriving plants may struggle. The skilled gardener doesn't abandon the entire plot when these challenges arise. They observe, adapt, and try novel approaches. Similarly, your creative practice will evolve as your capacity, interests, and circumstances shift. This isn't failure, it's responsiveness.

Liberation comes when we release our grip on external validation and arbitrary benchmarks of success. Plants don't bloom to impress neighbors or win competitions. They bloom because that is what they naturally do when properly tended.

Your creativity, too, exists not to meet others' expectations, but as an authentic expression of your unique experience in the world. When we create from this place of authenticity rather than performance, our work carries a resonance that connects deeply with those who need precisely our perspective.

As you continue this journey, I invite you to periodically ask yourself:

- What is genuinely sustainable for me right now?
- What creative approaches bring me joy rather than depletion?
- Where might I experiment with new methods that better accommodate my actual capacity?
- How can I celebrate the creative growth that's happening, even when it looks different from conventional milestones?

Like spring itself, your creative awakening doesn't require perfect conditions or ideal circumstances. It requires only your willingness to show up as you authentically are, to plant what interests you in soil you can actually tend, and to trust the natural unfolding of your unique creative voice.

The world needs your stories — not despite but because of the diverse ways you experience and navigate reality. By liberating yourself from preconceived rules about how creation should happen, you make space for the unexpected beauty that emerges when we allow our creative practices to honor the full truth of our lives. This liberation isn't just personal, it's collective. Each time we validate unconventional creative approaches, we expand the possibilities for all storytellers whose paths don't follow traditional routes.

Your ongoing journey as a creator may not always be straightforward, but it will always be yours. And in that authenticity lies both the challenge and the profound gift of creating as exactly who you are.

ABOUT THE AUTHOR

Jessica White is a fiction author and story coach who helps neurodivergent, chronically ill, and disabled storytellers craft authentic stories while honoring their unique creative rhythms. Combining her decade of experience as founder of the 365 Writing Challenge and admin for several other writing communities with a degree in educational studies, she guides storytellers in healing their relationship with time, energy, attention, and space.

Through the Authors Apothecary, Jessica blends somatic awareness, seasonal living, and mindful creativity to support storytellers in crafting authentic stories. Her work draws from both professional expertise as a developmental editor and personal experience with ADHD and chronic illness. Her published works span multiple genres and publishing styles, including ghostwriting. As an editor and story coach, she's helped dozens of authors bring their stories to life, believing that storytellers are healers, caretakers, and stewards of possibility.

For more information, please visit.
www.AuthorsApothecary.coms

Printed in Great Britain
by Amazon